Managing
with Style

Managing with Style

and making it work for you

Henry O. Golightly

ILLUSTRATIONS BY RIC ESTRADA

amacom

A DIVISION OF AMERICAN MANAGEMENT ASSOCIATIONS

Library of Congress Cataloging in Publication Data

Golightly, Henry O
  Managing with style.

    1. Management. I. Title.
HD38.G622   658.4   76-51445
ISBN 0-8144-5435-6

© 1977 AMACOM
A division of American Management Associations,
New York. All rights reserved. Printed in the United
States of America.

First Printing

This book is dedicated to all the executives whose styles have contributed to the dynamics of business and industry.

Preface

EVERY manager has a style. That style may be effective in one job but not in another. In fact, changing circumstances may turn a good style into a bad one. The basis of the approach taken in this book is that the manager's style may not be good or bad in itself—it is in the match-up of *style* with *task* that results are achieved or lost.

By implementing the concepts and recommendations discussed in the following chapters, a manager can analyze the style of executives who report to him or to her, detect weak spots, and take corrective action. When an executive is being considered for hiring, promotion, or transfer, the consideration of style can be a vital factor in predicting success. And the manager can use the concept to look at his own performance in order to make himself a more effective executive. Moreover, he can examine his boss's style with an eye toward establishing the best possible relationship with him.

During my many years as a consultant I have noted the growing tendency to comment on management performance in terms of style. At one time I accepted the assumption that "style," in this context, was merely a handy term to refer to various aspects of an executive's ability and personality, without having any particular meaning or importance of its own. Closer study led me to the feeling—and ultimately the conviction—that the concept of management style is a distinct and important factor in executive performance. For some time I have been observing and evaluating managers in terms of style—and I find that the approach works.

The study of style in management does not involve the introduction of previously unknown elements. It is, rather, a new and useful way of looking at the executive and the executive job. Management style offers us a useful way of analyzing an executive's effectiveness and of pinpointing and correcting problems. There is, however, an even more valuable aspect to the stylistic approach. When used properly, it offers to industry (and to institutions) a workable means of predicting performance.

Within this book we will establish a definition of management style and build a plan for perfecting it. We will determine its importance, explore the range of executive styles, spotlight methods of diagnosing defects, and consider the various points at which style affects the job.

I have tried to support my arguments by liberal use of anecdotes and case histories. Undoubtedly some readers will notice the absence of women in these little vignettes. My defense is that in the course of my experience, I met almost no women managers, which reflects the obvious fact that all too few women have been elevated to the managerial ranks. I have no doubt that as that situation changes, women will fit into both the strong and the weak patterns I have described in this book. Probably they will add some new twists as well.

I hope and believe that the manager who accepts the concept of style as a serious element in executive performance will find a new and sharp tool to help him carry out his vital responsibilities.

Henry O. Golightly

Contents

1—

What Is Management Style?

IN thousands of companies today, managers are in trouble. Their jobs and their careers are slipping away; things are going wrong, and they don't know what to do about it.

They're not stupid. Some of them can be found among the brightest executives in leadership positions today. Their backgrounds and track records are impeccable. They're not unprepared for responsibility, and they're not overly hampered by restrictions. They have every chance to succeed—but they are sinking.

You see it happen all the time. A manager with outstanding credentials moves into a demanding job. He seems to be trying to do all the right things, but the things he does don't pan out well. He—and the people who placed him in the job—grow increasingly frustrated and impatient because they can't figure out why this manager should be failing.

In a great many cases the root of the problem does not lie in lack of experience, energy, intelligence, or dedication. It stems from a factor often overlooked in analyzing the performance of executives: It's not enough to be prepared for your job and to work hard at it—*your style has to be right*.

Many executives dismiss management style as having little or no consequence. When they think about the subject at all, they regard style as a facade.

So before we discuss style, we must determine whether or not there is such a thing in management and, if there is, whether it amounts to anything important. This involves defining style in a business context, something that isn't as simple as it might first appear.

The concept of style seems to be rooted in writing. The word comes from the Latin *stilus,* the pointed iron or bone instrument used by the Romans to write on their waxen tablets. But its meaning has broadened to include a wide range of human thought and activity. The applicable dictionary definitions today are "specific or characteristic man-

*Every manager's style
is different.*

ner of expression, execution, construction or design, in any art, period, work employment, etc. . . . *the way in which anything is made or done.*"

That last phrase comes close to the sense we are reaching for. Style in management is *the way in which managing is done.* Nevertheless, our definition is not yet complete. To put a handle on the word and the concept that it conveys, we will have to examine some of the things that management style does *not* mean. So let's take a look at some common misconceptions about the notion of style as it applies to executives.

Style is just something that exists on the surface.

Jackson, a marketing vice president for a consumer goods firm, sits behind his desk and stares across at three key product managers. Perhaps "sits" is not exactly the right word for what Jackson is doing; he *crouches.* There is a pregnant silence. One of the product managers hesitantly clears his throat and then begins to outline a campaign, stumbling over his words and watching the boss closely as he goes along. Jackson's cobra-like stare never leaves the manager's face.

Then Jackson speaks: "Pete, you might have something there, or you might not. The point is, who the hell knows? Where's the research to underpin your assumptions? You haven't got the numbers to back them up. In this business we can't afford to go off half-cocked."

The product manager explains he had thought they could talk over the general idea before deciding whether to go into it more deeply with a market study, but Jackson waves this excuse aside with a lordly gesture. The product manager knows that if he had called for any substantial amount of research before springing the plan, Jackson would have been equally caustic about spending time and money on an idea before getting reactions to it; but this knowledge does not help the product manager much. He subsides into silence, and Jackson waits for the next batting-practice pitcher to throw one down the middle so he can belt it over the fence.

Jackson is acting according to a style. At this point we won't attempt to analyze his style—that's a topic to be considered later—but we need not be very perceptive to conclude that it is pretty negative. However, there is one thing we can say: Jackson's style is not just a superficial characteristic. His behavior reflects something that is fundamental in his nature and his approach to running his business. Furthermore, it has a profound effect on the way his division operates. We don't have to know all about the firm to conclude that the chances for real creativity from this group of product managers are slim. And in any business—but particularly in consumer goods—that's bad news.

Style is more than a surface manifestation. The point can be brought home sharply by looking at architecture for an analogy. Consider the differences between the Gothic and Byzantine styles. Their respective use of space, materials, ornamentation, and many other elements grew out of basic differences in construction and technology, but also they reflected the approaches to life of the people of the time and the rulers who led them. Similarly, a manager's style grows out of his basic approach to his job and his career and has a broad and deep influence on the performance and the future of the operation that he runs.

Style is something you find in some people but not in others. You either have it or you don't.

Not true. Let's take a look at two managers we'll call Porter and Wynn:

Porter is tall and good looking. His voice is deep, his gaze is penetrating. When he talks, people listen, and when he walks, people watch. He makes decisions with dash and communicates them with impact. Porter is very good one-on-one. He is a persuasive talker. Colleagues and subordinates come out of meetings with him realizing that they have agreed to things they had no intention of agreeing to when they went in. Furthermore, Porter is a compelling public speaker, frequently in demand at company gatherings and industry conventions. He is "good copy," often quoted in trade publications.

By contrast, Wynn is a quiet, unobtrusive man, not exceptionally noticeable in a crowd, he does a lot of listening. He speaks softly, his voice so low so that you sometimes have to strain to hear him. Wynn's memos are sensible, not an exhilarating literary experience for the reader. Subordinates feel that he lets them alone and gives them maximum latitude, maybe too much. At a convention, Wynn is just a man with a name tag on his lapel. At restaurants, headwaiters tend to seat him near the kitchen.

People say of Porter, "That guy has style!" They don't say that about Wynn. The consensus is that Wynn has no style.

That consensus is wrong. It confuses distinctiveness and conspicuousness with style. The fact is that Wynn has every bit as much style as Porter. His unobtrusiveness, which is part of his makeup, stems from his basic structure, and his unspectacular style has just as much influence on the conduct of his job and on the people around him as Porter's flamboyant style has on his job and people.

Writers and critics know that the seeming absence of style is a style in itself. Thousands of writers have worked hard to perfect a style that is so unobtrusive it does not show at all; only the meaning comes through. Somerset Maugham was one. He said, "A good style should show no sign of effort. What is written should seem a happy accident." (Of course, not every writer sees it that way.."In matters of grave importance," Oscar Wilde said, "style, not sincerity, is the vital thing.")

Some managers manifest a style that the onlooker is aware of all the time. Others seem to have no style at all. But this is misleading—a "low profile" is a style too.

You can change your style to suit the situation.

There is just enough truth in this one to make it dangerously illusory. A person can, by constant and deliberate effort, appear to adopt a different style from the one that is naturally his own. If he works hard at it, he can get away with it for a while. But over any period of time, under the stress of management responsibility, the attempt to mimic an alien style will fail. People are not chameleons. And even if, like those interesting lizards, they were able to take on new colorations, they would be changing only the surface, not the substance.

A manager who tries to assume a foreign style and apply it consistently to all aspects of his job will run into trouble for reasons that are shown by the following example.

Rudley was a tough guy; some said he was ruthless. When he was young he went to work for a company in which dog-eat-dog was the norm, and this environment suited Rudley to a T. He wheeled and dealed in the jungle of intrigue. He was tough

7

in pressing an advantage and ungracious in conceding a mistake. He pushed people around and said what was on his mind, no matter who got hurt. And his native talent emerged through the form of this rugged style. He would not have won any popularity contests, but he accomplished some remarkable feats in building a lackluster division into a money-maker.

At last Rudley felt that he had gone as far as he could in that firm. Acceding to the persuasion of a search consultant and the consultant's client, Rudley took a more responsible job with a bigger outfit. He drove a hard bargain, but his track record made him seem worth it to his new employers.

By no means an unobservant man, Rudley soon figured out that the atmosphere in his new company was altogether different from that in which he had previously flourished. People did not routinely stab each other in the back. There was competition, yes, but it was gentlemanly. Subordinates were persuaded, not ordered. Mistakes were analyzed, not condemned.

Rudley decided that since he was in Rome, he had better do as the Romans were doing. His naturally belligerent nature chafed at what seemed to him to be the flabbiness of these particular Romans. Nevertheless, he felt he had no choice. And so Rudley adopted all the trappings of a style for which he had had little use and no respect in the past. He held his temper and responded in sympathetic tones when something displeased him. He gritted his teeth and set out to look for the good qualities in his subordinates instead of denouncing their faults. He carried on interchanges with every pretense of hearty civility. He smiled a lot.

Superficially, the charade was working. The only trouble was that this wasn't Rudley's natural style. He poured so much effort into the attempt to seem pleasant and accommodating that he was often not at peak capacity. Not knowing how to criticize without being harsh, he sometimes failed to criticize at all and let mediocre performance go by without comment.

Even though his performance was in many ways an expert acting job, the masquerade was not entirely successful. People in the company found no specific reason to take exception to his conduct, but they remarked that "there's something about

8

him. . . ." In stressful situations the ever-present smile just didn't seem appropriate. They couldn't put a finger on it, but they suspected that there was something phony. (And those who were aware of his reputation as a jungle fighter *knew* there was something phony.)

None of this would have mattered very much if Rudley's performance had been objectively excellent, but the inhibitions he imposed on his native style were working against him. He was not a success, and the day came when he was let go.

Styles must match needs and circumstances. General George Patton's style got him into a lot of trouble in World War II, so much so that it seemed he was finished as a commander. But that style was absolutely perfect for the monumental task of turning the Third Army around and smashing through to defeat the Germans in the Battle of the Bulge.

Dwight D. Eisenhower, on the other hand, did not possess the style that would have made him a field commander of Patton's stature in that critical situation. But the Eisenhower style was ideally suited to the Herculean task of Supreme Commander, reconciling all the conflicting views and demands that made the strategy conferences of the Allies such a donnybrook of infighting and intrigue. In your mind's eye reverse the roles and speculate on how the Eisenhower style might have worked in the field in the winter of 1944, and how the Patton style would have done over at Supreme Headquarters. Not very successfully.

A final misconception: *Style does not make much difference if you know what you're doing.*

Managerial know-how is valuable only when it is expressed in action, and that expression in action is a function of style. Take the case of Brown.

An excellent financial man, Brown had come up through the ranks from accountant to reach the treasurer's chair. Brown had not permitted his specialty to blind him to other aspects of the business. He had been an assiduous observer and had picked up a thorough knowledge of the business. He was the natural choice for chief executive when the job opened, and he was given the promotion.

At this time the company had come to a crucial fork in the road. It would be necessary to make some hard and clear-cut choices about the direction the organization was going to take, and those choices would in turn dictate some fundamental decisions about marketing and manufacturing as well as financing. Brown knew what he was doing, all right; his grasp of the broad view and the details of each major branch of the firm was impressive. But he could not seem to bring himself to make the critical choices.

The difficulty was not lack of knowledge, ability, or insight; it was style. Brown's style impelled him by nature to be an "averager." If a heavy bet had to be placed on one horse, his instinct was to lay it off on another. Although this style had stood him in good stead for years, now there was no more room to hedge the bets. Definite decisions had to be made. But it was not part of Brown's style to make them, and he straddled so long that opportunities were lost and the company began to slide into a decline.

Management style is not just something that exists on the surface, unrelated to what is going on underneath. It is not something that some people have and others lack, nor is it a mode of behavior that can be adopted and changed at will. "A man's style," said Maurice Valency, "is intrinsic and private with him like his voice or his gesture, partly a matter of inheritance, partly of cultivation. It is more than a pattern of expression. It is the pattern of the soul." Georges Buffon, the eighteenth-century French critic, put it more simply: "The style is the man himself."

You have a style of management, whether others notice it or not. It is a reflection of what you are, and it has significant effects on what you do and how well you do it. These facts can be translated into the following working definition: *Management style is a combination of characteristics that indicates what a person is, influences the things he does, and controls the effectiveness with which he does them.*

Every manager has his own style, but this in itself does not make style important. Every manager has a navel, too.

Is style important? And if so, what makes it important? Let's look in on a boardroom. This episode actually happened. It is typical of many others in my experience.

The executive committee has met to nominate a new president. There is one leading candidate, who is highly qualified in every respect—except one. After some discussion of the candidate's outstanding record, intellect, integrity, and standing in the industry, the chairman says: "But this man doesn't have any *style.*"

The chairman has put his finger on what to him is the candidate's Achilles' heel. What he really means is that the candidate's style is different from that of the outgoing president, and that that difference would be critical in determining how the candidate would run the company. The incumbent is tough, a despot in many ways, but he has a kind of flair. People don't like him, but they follow him.

The man under consideration is well liked. He is quiet, cooperative, understanding. But he doesn't have the qualities that the chairman feels are needed behind the president's desk. The others on the executive committee agree, and a candidate with a lot going for him is passed over.

The decision was not made on the basis of brains, or background, or track record. Style was the critical factor. It can mean the winning or losing of a key promotion, and even the success or failure of a career.

There's something else about style. Doing his job should be *fun* for the manager. If a manager doesn't enjoy his job, he won't do it well. Style, and variations in style, makes management an interesting and diverting practice. Without it, management would be a dull business, lacking vitality, individuality, personality, and the human touch.

Imagine a company where all the managers have been replaced by computers (an obvious impossibility, but imagine it for a moment anyway). These computers perform the essential management tasks: They accept input, collate it, formulate plans, make decisions. It's all done by the numbers. Subordinates approach the machine and feed in data, receiving in turn directives in the form of printouts. The computers never laugh or joke, or get mad, or go out for lunch or a drink. They have no personality; they have no *style*. Such a business would be unimaginably boring. It might conceivably be efficient, but it would not be fun.

Few of us work for money alone. We get satisfaction from the job—or if we don't, we wish we did.

If a person is stuck in an organization where he doesn't feel comfortable, or where he isn't given the scope he needs, the problem may be one of style. For example, consider this executive:

Windsor joined a company as a senior vice president. He had studied the company thoroughly, concluded that it was going places, and decided that his abilities would fit well into the company's plans.

Windsor was right up to that point. His abilities fitted in well, but he had not gone deeply enough into the question of style. Windsor was highly organized and well disciplined. He liked to arrange his day meticulously, assigning blocks of time to each activity. He tolerated little or no deviation from schedule. In his previous jobs he had been able to order things the way he wanted them.

In the new job this was impossible. There were a lot of talented people in the leadership echelons, but most of them seemed to operate on a different wavelength from his. They came in at all hours of the morning, often as late as 11 o'clock, and they worked until late at night. Important meetings frequently didn't start until 6:30. Windsor, who liked to go home and relax over a cocktail before a leisurely dinner, didn't feel at his best over a corned beef sandwich and a plastic container of coffee.

Windsor's lack of adjustment to the style of his colleagues soon became evident. The others talked about him and kidded him. They respected his thinking, but they regarded him as odd, a little square. Some people wouldn't have been bothered by this, but it bothered Windsor. He didn't feel that he could continue in such an alien atmosphere. At last he managed to land a job in another organization. It didn't seem to be skyrocketing toward industry domination, but he felt comfortable.

This kind of stylistic lack of fit can work the other way around. I have seen freewheeling executives who have gone to new jobs with high hopes only to chafe impatiently within what seemed to them to be a hidebound and restrictive atmosphere. Such ill-positioned managers have not lost their ability or their faculties. They are victims of stylistic incompatibility. Enjoyment of a job—or lack of it—is largely a matter of the matching of styles.

Style—the personal styles of individuals, and the collective style of a company—can be a useful source of information. A manager considering a position with a firm can ask questions and learn many of the basic facts about the company—compensation, fringe benefits, the financial position, the job description—but there is no way to look at numbers and get a feel for the place. This must be gotten from exposure to style. For instance, if the job candidate finds that most of the people he talks with seem relaxed, outspoken, and genially irreverent about the company, he may reasonably conclude that this is the dominant style of the place.

The candidate will do well to consider whether he feels comfortable with these people and this style, or whether he would have to make considerable adjustments in his own style to get along in the new place. His instinct may tell him that however attractive the offer, he would never be altogether at ease there. This instinct may well be correct. Style conditions the working atmosphere, and if you have a job that requires constant adjustment of your stylistic thermostat, you are probably in the wrong spot.

And style is a telltale indicator of the kind of company you may be dealing with. This is not true just for job seekers, but for customers and for a lot of others outside the organization. One man says to another, "I'm thinking of making a deal with Amalgamated. Know anything about them?" The other replies, "Yes. They've done some good things, but they're a sloppy outfit when it comes to details."

There is an even more vital facet of style than those discussed thus far: the effects of personal style on executive performance. Let's take one fundamental aspect of the manager's job and look at the relationship between style and effectiveness.

Theoretically, decision making is a clean, cold science. The manager collects pertinent data, sketches out alternative courses of action, projects the consequences of each course, and then chooses what he considers the best plan. When we put it this way, it's difficult to see what style has to do with the process. But decisions are made in the real world. Take the case of manager Frank Green:

Green is perceptive and has a sharp mind. He works coolly under pressure. He is able to accept the realities of a situation. When faced with a decision, he grasps the critical factors and considers all the alternatives.

Green's style comes into play when it's time to choose an alternative. A "close to the vest" man, Green tends to keep a low profile and to make as few waves as possible. The solution that emerges from his deliberations may be a sweeping and spectacular plan, but he will pick away at it until he has discovered a flaw. He will magnify that flaw, conclude that the course of action involves too great a risk, and settle for a "safer" and more modest answer. The elements of the decision-making process have not been short-circuited, but his style steers him away from what may objectively be the best course of action.

Just as style can lead to the *wrong* decision, it can gum up the implementation of the *right* decision by preventing the manager from mobilizing people into an effective force for execution of policy:

Wilcox and Decker are managers of sales divisions within the same company. Both are experienced and capable, but their respective styles are in sharp contrast. Wilcox is an outgoing, backslapping type. He enjoys sitting around and swapping stories with the salesmen. The men like him; they consider him one of the boys.

Decker is a more reserved, numbers-oriented manager. He insists on meticulous call reports (Wilcox doesn't pay all that much attention to them). Decker likes to analyze situations rather than think about people. His men admire his grasp of product and competitive knowledge and his ability to think tough problems through, but they don't warm up to him.

For some years the company's sales effort centered on a multitude of low-level retail outlets. Volume was principally a matter of hustling, making the calls, and establishing strong personal relationships. Wilcox's division consistently led Decker's in the monthly figures. Decker planned the operations of his division better, but Wilcox was able to evoke a personal loyalty from his men that led to that little extra effort.

Then the firm introduced some new products that required a different kind of selling. The average sale became a negotiated deal, with the contract calling for much more money than before. The callback routine extended over a much greater period. This new type of selling called for a reorientation of the salesmen, and the burden of retraining fell on the division managers.

Wilcox immediately ran into problems. The new requirements were unpopular with a lot of salesmen, particularly the veterans. Since they considered Wilcox one of the boys, they assumed that he felt the same way they did, no matter what his job required him to say. Furthermore, Wilcox's easygoing style did not make him an effective trainer.

Decker, on the other hand, had never been one of the boys. His salesmen thought of him as a tough-minded, analytical thinker. Whether they liked him or not, they felt that he understood the new setup and that he could be a real source of help in making the switch. Rather than waste time in complaining about the new arrangement, the salesmen listened while Decker discussed the new problems and suggested angles of attack. His division soon moved out ahead of Wilcox's in the sales figures.

There is little difference between Wilcox and Decker in terms of intelligence and ability to size up new situations. Wilcox knew as well as Decker what had to be done. But his style, which had stood him in good stead throughout much of his career, had bestowed on him an image that hampered his ability to turn his division around. Decker, on the other hand, had been handicapped earlier by his cold, cerebral style. But when the nature of the sale changed so that it required more system and less personality, his men saw him as a leader who could help them cope.

Style is not in itself a management skill, but it conditions the ways in which management skills are exercised. To some degree this happens because a style imposes some limitations. It happens, also, because a particular style leads other people—colleagues and subordinates—to form a particular perception of a manager.

There is no facet of management skill that is not touched in some way by style. The function that would seem to be most remote from stylistic influence is that of planning—not the execution of plans but the act of planning itself. After all, since planning is a matter of concentration, analysis, and vision, how can the personal style of an executive influence his ability to plan effectively? The answer is that planning also depends on the amount and quality of input received by the planner, and the acquisition of input is heavily influenced by style:

Fred Atherton is planning some plant changes so that a new line of products can be manufactured, assembled, and shipped. Atherton is a loner who works with charts and figures. He looks at the factory plan and ruthlessly slashes through walls and repositions work groups. Given the kind of input Atherton is working with, his changes are logical.

Another manager, Gross, is in the same situation. Gross knows all about the need for a free flow of materials, smooth feed of subsidiary lines into the main assembly area, and so forth. But, unlike Atherton, Gross possesses a congenial, democratic style. He spends time talking to foremen and rank-and-file workers. He gets around the plant.

Gross's style opens up for him a source of input that is closed to Atherton. He senses that the moves that look most logical on paper may not work out well in practice, because the human beings involved may resent being moved around like pins on a map. And so Gross's rearrangement of the plant takes the human factor into account.

There is no real difference between Atherton and Gross in intelligence, experience, or appreciation of the necessities of the planning process. The difference lies in the different types of input elicited by their styles.

So style is more than just the factor that lends zest to the manager's job and conveys an image of manager and company to these on the outside. It is a medium that influences how the manager uses each of his skills.

And the manager's style influences in turn those who report to him. Look at an organization, be it a department, a division, or an entire company. The way people work, the attitudes they take, the ideas they express, and the efforts they make are all conditioned by the style of the individual who runs the show. If a new boss with a different style takes over, the change doesn't take long to make itself visible. Some people try to modify their styles and their actions to conform with the new regime. Others find that their status in the organization seems to have grown or diminished, not because their abilities have changed but because their styles fit better or worse. Some of these people will stay; others will leave. The style of the manager is far from the only factor in the makeup of an organization, but it certainly is a major influence.

Obviously, style is important, important enough to warrant some serious thought. Our next step is to proceed to an analysis of the various types of management style.

2 -

The Spectrum of Management Styles

THERE is a wide variety of management styles. Most have some good points and some bad points. There is no "pure" style. Each executive brings to the job his own particular blend of management traits, which add up to his style. Some of the traits in his style will coincide with those in other styles, even some that are on the whole quite different. But each approach usually has one dominant characteristic that places it at one point along the style spectrum and distinguishes it from the others. This dominant trait gives flavor to the way the manager works and the ways in which others react to him.

On the basis of such dominant traits, we can identify ten prevalent management styles. They are:

Management by inaction
Management by detail
Management by invisibility
Management by consensus
Management by manipulation
Management by rejection
Management by survival
Management by despotism
Management by creativity
Management by leadership

In this chapter we will examine those ten styles. We will see how one style sometimes blends into another, and how a certain style can be disguised as another. And we will consider the question of the best style for each manager.

Management by Inaction

The inactive style has a number of interesting variations. The extreme form is characterized by inertia:

Charles Eidler sits in a meeting with three key subordinates. They have been discussing a problem. Eidler says, "What do you think we ought to do about this, Sam?" Sam speaks his piece. Then Eidler turns and asks, "What's your slant on it, Joe?" Joe puts in his two cents. Finally, "Pete, how do you stand?" And Pete relates what he thinks ought to be done. Eidler sits there for a while, looking thoughtful. (One attribute possessed by most inactive managers is that they are able to look thoughtful even when they are not thinking.) Then: "Well, let me mull this over and we'll see where we come out."

"Where we come out" is usually no place. In the absence of any direction—by this time they are used to it—Sam, Joe, and Pete cope with the problem as best they can. A week later they convene again for another exercise in inertia.

The inertial, or do nothing, style is not a way to run a business for very long, but there are situations in which it can work, at least for a while. When the operation is rolling along with fairly healthy success and a minimum of problems, doing nothing is better than constant tinkering. But few of us are lucky enough to be in spots where we can get away with management by inertia.

The *mañana* style is different from total inertia in that the manager is willing to admit the possibility that something is going to have to be done sometime. He simply delays it as long as possible:

President Will Waite admitted that something had to be done about the Blodgett Division. The division was outmoded, it presented endless logistic problems, it was losing effectiveness. Waite admitted that something had to be done every time his top subordinates faced him with the problem.

But Will Waite was a master of delay. He would appoint task forces, set up study groups, call for research, and refer to "forthcoming developments" that would "fit the last piece into the puzzle" and clear the way for action.

22

*Knowing your own style
may determine your success.*

The only action that was forthcoming, however, was Waite's departure on a leisurely vacation. In his absence, *mañana* arrived. His subordinates gathered in a rump session, came to a conclusion, and went to the chief executive. The CEO forced action on Waite and, not long thereafter, forced him out of the company.

There's a modification of the inactive style that permits action—as long as the action is taken by others:

Forbush is a financial manager in a large corporation. He is a tireless collector of data; the computer memory bank is superfluous when he is around.

Forbush can provide you with any statistic you want. Operating managers go to him when they are stuck for a number. But Forbush only provides his data to others for their use; he never uses them himself. Sometimes he doesn't wait to be asked. When a situation becomes desperate enough, Forbush begins to leak information. In the middle of a conversation with the president, for example, he will produce some figures from left field. "What does it mean?" asks the president. With a show of utmost reluctance, Forbush might vouchsafe that the figures seem to suggest that somebody in that division is not very profit minded.

Action will ensue; but Forbush won't have any part in it. He boasts that he has "never had a confrontation" with a manager from another division.

(Beware the financial man who does not have confrontations; a good financial man can be expected to have at least one confrontation every day.)
Sometimes it takes a lot of effort to see that nothing gets done:

Jed Ringling is a ball of fire in the conference room. He dominates the discussion with lengthy speeches. He digresses articulately and entertainingly. He regales the meeting with the latest stories, which he tells very well. On the occasions when a subordinate manages to get the floor to present a suggestion, Ringling seizes on the suggestion with enthusiasm, spins it in the air, does dazzling tricks with it.

The only trouble with all this is that people leaving the meeting look at each other and ask, "What happened?" The answer is usually, "Nothing."

You can frequently spot the dynamic inactivist. He sits behind a palisade of paper piles. He zooms from one subject to another with amazing swoops of logic. He interrupts himself to go off on a tangent. Subordinates do not know what they themselves are doing most of the time.

Paul Zareba was a master stylist of confusion. Curiously enough, the fouled-up state of Zareba's organization served, at first, as a magnet for promising subordinates. Zareba would tell a potential recruit that things were in bad shape and that he needed some fresh blood to help him clean things up. Many executives went for this bait. They were attracted, also, by Zareba's vow that they were the heirs apparent to Zareba's job. (In this one thing Zareba was consistent; he made the same promise to each new manager who joined him.)

The organization chart meant nothing. Zareba would assign someone to an area and then assign someone else to an overlapping area. Two or three executives would find themselves bumping into each other on a typical Zareba project. When they went to the top to get things cleared up, they were met with one of the finest double-talk acts since the heyday of vaudeville.

Turnover was high. After a while, disgusted managers would leave Zareba's bedlam. Some stayed, managed to get used to the chaos, and even worked out ways to get things done. Zareba was not without native ability, and his empty promises were effective—for a time—in bringing in good talent. But at last the confusion turned on its creator. Zareba is not in business anymore.

The inactive style grows out of fear and uncertainty. It may also grow out of boredom. In general, the inactive manager is the kind of congenital optimist who figures that if you ignore a problem, it will go away, or at least get better.

Some naturally inactive managers camouflage their styles. They adopt the trappings of activity, either because they know that this is the route to the top or because they are caught in situations where inactivity would be ludicrously inappropriate. But when they reach a point where they can indulge their natural tendencies, the true colors are hoisted and they lapse into a corporate coma.

The inactive style can work pretty well for a while in some spots, usually areas of the business where there is a set routine and things run themselves fairly well. Marketing, however, where things are constantly changing, is definitely not such a spot. It's the worst possible place for an executive to practice the inactive approach.

Sooner or later the inactive manager runs into difficulty. Sometimes in fact, the hands-off attitude permits problems to grow into disaster. For example, a few years ago a midwestern company bought a number of small businesses throughout the country. These acquisitions marketed similar product lines. The objective was to funnel all the products through the parent's strong distribution system, but the subsidiaries objected. Faced with this opposition, the president did nothing. Finally the board insisted that the original plan be implemented, but not before millions had gone down the drain.

This example points up another common reason for inaction. Doing things is not only risky; it may be unpopular. To keep in everyone's good graces, the executive does nothing. But, in the end, the inactivist is usually forced to "Do something—even if it's wrong." And often it *is* wrong. Since he is not used to action, he is clumsy at it and his hasty moves miss the mark.

The proponent of inactivity is usually left behind in the fast-moving world of modern business. He would do better in a more solitary occupation.

Management by Detail

Dan Weise, the vice president for production of a large manufacturing firm, is a painstaking collector of data. Weise's colleagues are used to hearing him say, "First let's get the facts." Weise gets the facts whenever he is confronted by the need to make a plan or a decision. He patiently amasses bits of information until he has a substantial pile. And he keeps rearranging these bits of information to establish new patterns.

This is the methodical style of management. The exponent of the methodical style cannot be hurried. He wants to make sure, and his way of making sure is to see that he has available to him every conceivable fact that may bear—even remotely—on the situation.

Management by detail has its strong points. It is a way of imposing order on complex situations. The methodical manager rarely overlooks any really important factor. By making an orderly, infinitely detailed analysis of a situation, he assures himself of being in touch with all its facets. His decisions are the products of agonized labor.

Nevertheless, there are problems with this style. The overly methodical manager is apt to act too late. And even when he does not act too late, his action may be timid and inappropriate. Management by detail is seductive in that there never is a time when the executive cannot call for more information—and more and more. Electronic data processing, with its endless capacity for generating data and offering varying breakdowns, makes it easy for this type to satisfy his appetite.

The methodical manager is in danger of losing sight of the forest because he has become too absorbed in his painstaking examination of the trees. The manager who is trying to fit hundreds of small pieces of information into a pattern may lose vision and perspective.

Management by Invisibility

The invisible manager does not just avoid activity; he stays out of sight. Getting access to him is an adventure. And, when a determined subordinate does manage to win through and confront the boss, the boss might as well be invisible.

There are reasons for a manager's adoption of the invisible style. It may even serve to protect him from his own faults. For example, take the case of Jack Blade.

As Blade started up the ladder, he was a normally visible young executive with a sharp mind and developing skills. But along with that sharp mind, he was cursed with an equally sharp tongue.

When Blade went to work for the Clamm Company, he handled his first assignment well. When the president approached him with another project, one he didn't think much of, Blade bluntly told the president, "You're crazy!" For some reason the president took offense, and it was not long before Blade was fired. From that time on, he has cultivated the invisible style. He assigns people to tasks and then gets out of the picture and stays out.

A tendency toward extreme bluntness is one reason for donning the cloak of managerial invisibility. Another is shyness; some executives feel a lot more comfortable with numbers than with people.

Still another factor can be intense preoccupation with priorities and the value of one's time. When you are visible, people stop to talk with you. If you think conversation is a time waster, you can avoid it by maintaining invisibility.

The invisible style can work. It has its advantages. When the boss remains offstage, there is more limelight for his subordinates. Those who are highly motivated by recognition feel that they can get their full share of it.

When the top brass is never around, subordinates are certainly called upon to develop resourcefulness and self-reliance. They will think their decisions through and plan their actions in the knowledge that the boss is not going to come around to bail them out.

If, for any reason, a manager elects to run things by staying out of sight, he must be absolutely sure

he has the people to make it work and that they are
loyal to him and to the company.

Management by Consensus

Consensus can be very important, particularly
in assuring the harmonious execution of decisions.
Americans who deal with Japanese businessmen
for the first time are struck by what seems like
indecisiveness. The Japanese keep coming back,
meeting after meeting, without a decision. But,
when they do reach and announce a decision,
they have already achieved complete agreement
on its implementation.

The consensus style grows in importance as
subordinates acquire independence and power. In
such a decentralized organization as General Elec-
tric, for example, a companywide policy would be
in trouble if it failed to win the full approval of
group heads, who are practically autonomous. So
the consensus style has its advantages.

But consensus management is not so useful
when it grows out of the decision maker's fear of
taking action by himself. Some executives collect
agreement as a kind of security blanket. They want
to be able to say, "I've talked it over with my
people, and this is what we all agree." Some managers will do this even when the decision is one that
does not involve subordinate managers and should
be made by the top man alone.

Ernest Parr is a shining example of the consensus style at its worst:

Parr is the president of a medium-size company. His hallmark is the question, "What do you think?" A manager comes to Parr with an idea. Parr absorbs the suggestion, then tries it out on the other managers, singly or in groups. He does not stop at the management level; he has been observed "bouncing an idea off" the elevator starter and the man who comes around to shine his shoes.

The consensus method is not altogether bad, but Parr carries it to extremes. He spends so much time trying to get agreement that his key subordinates have established a pattern of their own. To save time and get something done, they will exchange ideas beforehand and then go to Parr as a unit to hand him a ready-made consensus.

Consensus is extremely important in setting policy, but it should not be a factor in making decisions within a policy. Once consensus in policy is reached, the manager should make the decisions that he alone can make, and should delegate those that he can delegate. There are few exercises that are more futile than the one in which a consensus-minded manager tries to make a decision by means of a meeting.

Management by Manipulation

All good managers are, to some degree, manipulators. In some circles it has become fashionable to look upon manipulation as something awful, to be avoided at all costs. But there are many kinds of manipulation, fair and unfair, effective and ineffective, legitimate and illegitimate.

Manipulation turns sour when it is done for its own sake rather than to achieve corporate goals, by a manager who just enjoys pulling the strings. When a puppet does not respond the way he thinks it ought to, that puppet is discarded.

People are not puppets—at any rate, good people are not. Independent and creative managers resent the feeling that they are merely subjects of the boss's will and they soon move elsewhere. The puppet master may keep an operation running for a while, as long as his strength and luck hold out, but he is trying to do it all himself. The people whom he transforms into puppets will not be able to help him when he needs help, and so he will fail.

The ineffectuality of the puppet-master style points up one important point about legitmate manipulation. If it is to work, manipulation must not be apparent to those who are being manipulated. The controls must be indirect and unobtrusive; the strings must be totally invisible.

Some manipulators are spellbinders:

Division manager Earl Fullerton is confronted by a subordinate who has just expressed strong disagreement with a plan that Fullerton has proposed. Fullerton won't use force, and he won't pull rank or pull strings, but he is determined to manipulate the subordinate into a position of compliance.

So Fullerton goes into his act. He speaks brilliantly and persuasively. His voice rolls out in pleasing cadences. It is a forceful and compelling performance, and at the end the subordinate is agreeing with everything Fullerton says. Later this same subordinate will try to figure out the exact sequence of argument and logic that won him over—and he won't be able to.

The spellbinder has undoubted gifts. Unfortunately, he frequently wastes those gifts by deploying them to manipulate people. He does not ask himself, "What is the best policy for us to follow?" He asks, "How can I get this guy to do what I want him to do?" Through personal power he is successful, for a while, in his efforts at manipulation. But ultimately everybody has seen his act, and they don't buy it anymore.

Then there is the fight-promoter approach. The manipulator fosters so much conflict among his subordinates that nobody can get along with anybody else. Adam Gore possesses such a style:

Looking over a proposal by one of his department heads, Gore says, "Maybe this will work, but how are you going to get Jess Raven to go along with it? Looks to me as if you're stepping on his toes. It will look that way to him, too."

The subordinate, not unnaturally, wants Gore to straighten out the conflict, if one really exists. But that's not Gore's way of doing things. "Now you guys had better settle this between yourselves." A little later, to add fuel to the flames, Gore asks Jess Raven, "Has Eddie talked to you yet about his plan? It kind of intrudes into your bailiwick, but maybe you fellows can work something out."

Gore manages to give each party the impression that he favors his side of the argument. When they arrive at the inevitable impasse, Gore is able to step in: "Since you guys weren't able to reach agreement, I guess I'll have to set something up. We can't go on fighting about it any longer." What Gore "sets up" is exactly what he wanted to do from the beginning.

The fight promoter likes to work this way. It keeps people off balance, and this gives him a feeling of superiority. It also keeps any single subordinate from accomplishing a great deal. When things go wrong, the manager can try to get off the hook with his own superiors by saying, "The plan was a good one, but with Eddie and Jess at each other's throats it didn't receive the proper execution. Something will have to be done about at least one of those men."

But any sense of security that the fight promoter gets is apt to be illusory. Since he is putting so much effort into fomenting trouble, and his subordinates are so hotly engaged in battling each other, bottom-line productivity is bound to decline.

There is a form of manipulation that involves the amassing of a fake consensus. The late Lyndon B. Johnson was fond of the word "consensus." He persuaded, cajoled, threatened—and came out with agreement. But the agreement that LBJ came out with was usually the desire that he went in with. He decided on action, then went around to his colleagues to let them know what their consensus was.

Another form of manipulated consensus grows out of undue concern with the notion of corporate democracy or participatory management:

Division head Fred Lee has been sitting around the conference table with his subordinates for two hours. There is a problem on the agenda. Lee goes from one man to another asking for suggestions, eliciting comments, trying for agreement.

The reason for this tortuous process is not that Lee does not know what to do. He knows exactly what to do. But he fears that just telling his key people what he is going to do would not be "democratic." So he goes through the wearying process of keeping the managers talking until they say what he wants them to say.

34

As Dr. Abraham Maslow, the pioneer of motivational psychology, has pointed out, this kind of imposed consensus is worse than a waste of time; it turns people off. Sooner or later they realize that the seeker of "consensus" is really trying to inseminate them with his own ideas.

The manager who uses positive manipulation might be called a "master builder":

John Ball is a highly successful president. A constructive manipulator, he uses manipulation not for its own sake or as a defensive measure, but in pursuit of clear goals. He manipulates to get the best out of people. For example, one of his subordinates is an ambitious man with a lot of talent, but he is hesitant about making decisions. This subordinate feels he is in competition with another man, who is decisive. So Ball pits one against the other, deliberately placing his indecisive subordinate in situations which force him to come up with answers.

Furthermore, Ball is fully aware that manipulation of people is a two-edged sword that must be used sparingly. So, when there is a choice, he prefers to manipulate circumstances so that his people operate better. When two valuable managers do not get along with each other, Ball neither encourages them to fight it out nor steps in to settle all arguments. To the extent possible, he structures their assignments so that they do not meet head-to-head in situations that lead to dispute.

The master-builder style requires that the manager use manipulation as a means to an end. He structures organization and procedure to foster maximum creativity and effort. He does not run his business as if manipulation were the only club in the bag.

Management by Rejection

Some managers operate with a thoroughly negative style. Their tendency is to say no rather than yes, to reject rather than accept.

Sessions with subordinates are one long exercise in batting practice. The manager says, in effect, "Pitch your idea over the plate and I'll slam it out of the park!" That gives you an idea of the way George Slaughter works.

The meeting opens with deceptive cordiality: "Well, let's get some thinking on the table. Who has a suggestion?"

Nobody is eager to be first; they've been through this before. So Slaughter selects some unfortunate soul to put forth recommendations, and then he wields his bludgeon: "Beautiful! That's one of those ideas that looks great when it's worked out in an ivory tower. But let's take a real close look at it. Do we ever stop to ask where the money is coming from?" And on and on, until the idea is thoroughly demolished.

Another idea is put forward. On this one, Slaughter changes his technique. He doesn't swing for the fences; he just bunts it to death. He says, "There may be some merit in what you say. I wonder if we can project some of the consequences. After all, if an idea has merit, it should be able to stand up to a test." Slaughter doesn't really rip into the suggestion, but after he has "projected the consequences" for 15 minutes, the recommendation has been gently clobbered.

It seems as if practically nothing ever gets through, and Slaughter's top subordinates have just about given up trying. "That S.O.B. doesn't want any ideas," one said angrily. "He's just a sadist." That may be a harsh judgment, but, whatever the reasons that underlie Slaughter's style, he is in trouble.

Some managers don't reject everything out of hand. They are selective:

Steve Bench was promoted to marketing vice president. He had not started in marketing but in operations. Nevertheless, Bench's qualifications had seemed overwhelming to the executive committee.

Bench did his best. He presented the facade of an energetic, outgoing type, although he was probably faking it a little. He established friendly relations with his selling and merchandising people. He used his operations savvy to straighten out some long-standing problems.

There was just one difficulty. Bench encouraged creativity, but he could not bring himself to accept anything that would involve spending a substantial amount of money. No matter how well the subordinate might document his case, something inside Bench's head went "click"—and the idea was turned off.

Other ideas—involving reorganization, or initiation of new procedures, on handling of personnel—he would judge with objectivity and perception. But the idea of spending money triggered his selective rejection mechanism. Although his managers would plead with him, "We're losing market share, we have to do something!" Bench would continue to reject anything with a sizable dollar price tag.

Sometimes his subordinates would get ideas past him. Once his sales manager, unable to get through to the vice president, took his case to the president—and won. Bench resented this. He said to the sales manager, "You know, it's possible to win a battle and lose the war." This turned out to be a self-fulfilling prophecy. Within six months he had fired the sales manager. But Bench himself did not last much longer.

Andy Keen is able to make the rejection style work by making himself a very tough customer—but not an absolutely impossible one. He acts as devil's advocate:

Keen approaches new suggestions with healthy skepticism. His initial inclination is to say no—and his subordinates are aware of this—but he waits. He keeps his mind open, concentrating on the idea and not on how he is going to destroy it.

So the subordinate who approaches Keen with a proposition knows that he had better be well prepared. He does his homework. He documents and tests his contentions. And he revs himself up to put the idea forward coherently and energetically, because he knows the boss is observing not only the inherent logic of the suggestion but the zeal of its inventor as well.

Most proposals that are put to Andy Keen are shot down—but not before a lively, fair debate takes place. Keen resorts to every conceivable argument to try to demolish the plan, but he does not hit below the belt. If the proponent of the idea is well prepared and his suggestion is good, he may win approval. This doesn't happen often, so it's stimulating and exciting when it does. Managers don't hesitate to approach Keen with ideas—they consider it a challenge, not a visit to the torture chamber.

The devil's advocate puts an essentially negative style to work by challenging his subordinates to do their best. In turn, he plays the game fairly by being willing to accept a proposal when the argument weighs heavily in its favor. In the devil's advocate style, not too many ideas get through, but those that do are apt to be winners.

Management by Survival

Certain executives calculate every move by its value as a technique for their personal survival. Their style is to do whatever is necessary to keep the job.

One extreme of the survival style is that of the jungle fighter:

Charley Venamen has the personality of a king cobra and is about as dangerous. He fought his way to the top of his company and was never deterred by a finicky regard for the rules of the game. Most managers play politics to some extent, but Venamen's version of politics is more like guerila warfare.

Venamen had been second in command of a large consumer goods firm. His far-flung grapevine brought him the information that the president was playing around with his secretary. Now this is not such a rarity, but Charley Venamen turned it into a major event. He managed to get the facts to the president's wife, an outspoken woman of considerable character. Lawyers and private detectives were brought into play; the mess got into the papers; the president became an embarrassment to the directors and was eased out. Charley took over.

Some managers espouse the gut-shooting style on the way up and then abandon it; not Charley. When he had no more superiors to plot against, he turned his tactics against his subordinates. "To make it here a man has to be tough," he boasts. (But not too tough; when a manager seems to be getting so adept at jungle fighting that he poses a threat to the boss, his head is lopped off.)

Charley's company is a nest of intrigue, and why not? The executives whom he promotes are low-caliber copies of himself. Unlike the fight promoter, Venamen does not sit above the battle. He is right there in the arena, still playing rough politics to the hilt.

Venamen and his staff are adept guerrillas—but so much of their combat is intramural that the fight against the competition is suffering. The board is beginning to notice, and Charley is not long for his job.

Some managers come naturally to the jungle-fighter style; others adopt it out of what they think is necessity. When it is applied with sufficient ruthlessness and skill, it can be a short-run career builder by eliminating competition for promotion. But it is essentially negative in the long run.

Playing a sharp game in company politics is an

element of business success. But the constructive management politician builds instead of destroying. He docs not glorify intrigue, nor does he invariably aim his best shots below the belt. A really good politician builds trust. He is not the kind of manager who assures a colleague he is not playing politics and a moment later shafts the colleague to the hilt.

The mirror image of the survivor is the executive whose aim in life seems to be to do what will be most popular with the greatest number of people:

Glen Reimer was a pleasant guy. Everybody liked him. He made his way up the corporate ladder easily and pleasantly. Nevertheless, when it came time to pick a new president, Glen's name was by no means at the top of the list. Each of the stronger candidates, however, had managed to make some enemies. It was felt that the new leader should be one who could "bring us together," so finally Glen Reimer was the compromise choice. Everybody, including Glen, was a little surprised when he got the job, but, except with the other candidates, it was a popular choice.

At the top, Glen continued to operate according to his Mr. Popularity style. When a key subordinate came in with a project he had his heart set on, Glen Reimer was a soft touch. Consequently the company began to establish beachheads in a great many areas—but all too often there were no beaches beyond those beachheads.

In the end they had to get rid of Glen Reimer. He has finally found a spot where he is not called upon to risk his popularity by making tough decisions.

The Mr. Popularity style is that of a survivor, not an accomplisher. The manager who is always trying to average out conflicting considerations to keep the largest number of people happy is a manager who can last quite a while—but not in a position of major responsibility. True high-level management involves the inevitable necessity of saying no and doing things that are not popular. It comes with the job title.

Management by Despotism

Some managers feel compelled to call all the shots. The totalitarian style is one in which the executive acts as ringmaster, performs all the acts, takes the tickets, and even sells the popcorn.

There are a number of interesting variations of the totalitarian style, all of them in evidence in executive suites today.

Dan Gross's approach is typified by the episode in which he hired a prominent economist at $100,000 a year:

The expert had not been on the job an hour when he was summoned to the chief's office. Gross introduced the subject of a new product line. The economist began to say that he would want to give the matter careful study before coming to any conclusions.

Gross waved this aside. "I don't give a damn what you think," he said. "This product line will have a growth rate of 7 percent and I want you to prove it."

This kind of despotic manager doesn't play politics with his subordinates, and he doesn't lead them into situations in which they destroy each other. If there is any destroying to do, he does it himself. No indignity is too great, no humiliation too

41

small to inflict on the people down the line. For example, in meetings Dan Gross always deliberately mispronounces the name of a certain manager—a man who has worked for him for four years!

The despot can make an organization move, all right. There is certainly not much confusion or clash of opinions. When he wants managers' opinions, he tells them what those opinions are.

But of course creative and independent people do not remain under such an aegis. Those who stay are apt to become extremely effective at carrying out orders. If they are not masochists—and there is more than a handful of these in the ranks of management—they become inured to insult and just do their jobs. They are likely to be well compensated. Attila the Hun pays good salaries; he has to.

Not all despots are raging tyrants. Some are benevolent.

Tom Smithers runs his department with an iron hand—but there are variations in the strength of his grip. For example, contrast these two examples of Smithers' style, displayed within an hour of each other:

Smithers meets first with Cal Blue, a veteran supervisor. Blue has been around a long time and has built up some experience and competence that has a certain value, but he is one of life's losers. Every now and then he tries something ambitious—and nearly always falls on his face. Just now he has loused up an assignment. Smithers listens to the talk of woe in silence. Then he says mildly, "Well, Cal, these things happen. It's not good. I hope we can avoid this kind of thing in the future." Cal leaves, wiping his brow.

Now for the next interview. Lee Winston is a young supervisor, bright and aggressive. Winston has not loused anything up; he has submitted a plan designed to improve operations. Smithers asks sardonically, "Lee, do you call this a proposal?" Not waiting for a reply, Smithers calls forth all his resources of sarcasm and derision to rip the plan apart. Winston leaves the office, crushed.

But in a few days there will be a sequel. Smithers will talk with Winston again, saying that he does see some elements of merit in the proposal—if a lot more work is done on it.

The benevolent despot is usually kind in dealing with the helpless and very tough on people who have something on the ball. He goes all out to knock them down but then he picks them up and brushes them off. They always "know who's boss."

But, benevolent or not, the despot likes to see people humbled:

One benevolent despot, a chief executive who was nearing the point at which he would step down, had his fun by hinting continually to each of four possible successors that he would be the chosen one. One of the heirs apparent was a despot more or less carved in the current boss's image. The other three candidates got together and let it be known that none of them would work for number four.

And of course the boss called them all in and announced that he was putting the miniature despot in charge. Instantly, one of the other three defected. He rushed to the new chief, clasped his hand, and exclaimed, "They could not have picked a better man." (The other two soon left the company.) This is the kind of episode that seems to make life worthwhile for the despotic manager.

Certain executives manifest a style distinguished by unrelieved arrogance. They base their despotism not on rank but on what they conceive to be innate superiority. It is more or less a latter-day resurrection of the concept of the divine right of kings.

The intellectual snob offers an interesting variation on the despotism theme. With his inherent tendency to be authoritarian, he does not wait until he is in charge to exercise his despotism. He is superior and condescending right from the start, to those he reports to as well as to his subordinates. And when the intellectual snob has the ability to underpin his style, he often gets away with it. Nobody likes him, but he is respected. Indeed, the person who seems to go out of his way to be abrasive often gains an exaggerated reputation for brilliance. ("He must have something on the ball to act like that.")

Regardless of their particular style, despotic managers never give anyone else credit for anything. The despot is apt to make good decisions—but his trouble comes when he tries to get people to carry out these decisions. To say the least, he does not have a lot of warm support.

There are times when authoritarianism is the best management style for running a particular organization. The despot can keep the ship on an even keel in a storm. When there is one-man rule, the organization can respond fast to emergencies and opportunities.

But there are drawbacks. Good people leave or are destroyed. The authoritarian manager makes enemies, and the seeds of animosity he sows can grow into a bitter harvest. (Labor relations are particularly exacerbated by this kind of handling.) And the authoritarian may become so complacent about his sovereignty that he resents the strong subordinate who is able to stand up to him.

The exponent of the authoritarian style can get things done, but he must be prepared to carry the whole load himself.

Management by Creativity

"It beats me how he does it. . . . "

A vice president, talking about his chief executive, continues: "You're sitting there with him. You've chewed over all the possible answers, but there doesn't seem to be any way out of the box. Then, all of a sudden, the light bulb seems to light up over his head. He jumps out of his chair and says, 'This is the way we'll handle it.' And he gives you a complete plan that seems to be made up out of thin air. But, you know, he's usually right. *That instinct is worth a million dollars.*"

The instinctive style can be spectacular. It impresses superiors, subordinates, and the world at large. It lends charisma to the manager who practices it. It confers an air of boldness and daring to the executive task. It cuts through nonessentials to the heart of a problem and produces striking and imaginative solutions.

Instinct can be invaluable in running a business *so long as it is soundly based on reality.* Unfortunately, not every executive who plays his hunches is able to muster the basic soundness that makes the approach work.

Here's a case in which instinct was not the answer:

For weeks the top executive team at Plethora Industries had been debating a vital decision. Two of Plethora's major competitors were moving into an important new marketing area. This posed a dilemma for the Plethora brass, and they were severely divided on how to resolve it. Some maintained that the company should stick to what it was doing now. Others insisted that Plethora had to move into the new field.

There was also considerable dispute among those who advocated expansion. They agreed that, to make the move, the company would have to acquire manufacturing and marketing capability. Some said this should be done by merger with one fairly large organization. Others stuck to the belief that Plethora would do better by acquiring three or four very small companies and combining their resources.

Plethora's president, Carl Sharp, spent days listening first to one side and then another. He asked penetrating questions and debated troublesome points—but gave no indication as to which way he was leaning. And then came the climactic moment. Sharp called his aides together and made the announcement: "We're not going any of the routes that have been discussed. We're going to do it another way. We'll expand—but we'll do it on our own; build our own plant and design and manufacturing team, and establish our own marketing apparatus."

Sharp's subordinates were awed. They had seen the chief operate by hunch before, but this decision dwarfed all previous instances. They asked questions about time and money, and Sharp had an answer for everything. Convinced that his bold solution was the best, he proposed to bleed resources from all operating departments to stake the new venture.

"I hope he's right," said one vice president.

"I expect he is," said another. "Those hunches of his have worked in the past."

Hopes and expectations were dashed. A year later the project had collapsed, Sharp was gone, and a less daring chief had been brought in to piece together the shards and remnants of the business.

Managers like Carl Sharp can be carried away by perverse instinct. Faced with alternatives that all seem to contain flaws, they turn instinctively to the sweeping resolution that nobody else has thought of. But beware of the instinct that impels you toward that one big stroke that solves all problems neatly. This is not an instinct for accomplishment but for escape, some way to get out of a bind, and the escape route usually leads up a dead-end street.

The instinctive style operates freely in decisions about people. The executive who would never make a move regarding equipment or plant without immersing himself in reams of data will respond to some individuals and mistrust others because of a feeling that wells up from the gut.

The ability to take gut readings of people is most valuable, but there are a lot more executives who think they are blessed with that wonderful ability than actually possess it. Past failures never deter them—they go on trusting their people instincts.

In hiring, a manager's misplaced confidence in his ability to evaluate human beings considerably increases his chances of choosing unwisely. It is this flaw on the part of some executives that allows certain kinds of managers to make lucrative careers at job getting rather than job doing.

For example, a fellow breezes into the office of the president. He speaks fluently and forcefully and has a "marvelous personality." On paper he may not look so good, but his version of the record makes him sound great. He maximizes his few successes and rationalizes away his numerous failures. If this president happens to be the "right" employer, our attractive loser will get a good job. In a couple of years his deficiencies will have caught up with him and he will be out looking for another job at even more money—and probably finding one.

The "right" employer for this fellow is the one who not only plays hunches about people but who bases those hunches on superficial indicators. Instinct for people is true and useful only when it gives a feel for what the person can do. When a manager bases his "instinct" on observation of cosmetic traits, he's not acting as an executive but rather as the judge at a personality contest.

Appraisal of people is a highly cultivated instinct. Businesses have been ruined by managers who place great confidence in the abilities of people they like or feel close to. This is carried to an extreme in the blood-is-thicker-than-water version of this style. A principal owner puts his son-in-law in charge of a going concern. In five years the unhappy father-in-law is selling at a big loss. The CEO of a toiletries company, looking around for somebody to redesign the packaging, picks his daughter. The daughter happens to have an affinity for pink, and soon the line is encased in hideous fuscia bottles, jars, boxes, and counter displays. Disaster engulfs the enterprise.

The most useful instinct is *trained* instinct.

The work of Picasso looks, to the undiscerning eye, like a jarring melange of distortions. The artist seemed to be following an instinct of his own—and so he was.

You will hear a spectator say, "My eight-year-old daughter could draw better than that." She couldn't. The artistic "hunches" of great artists are based on full command of the rules of the game. Picasso's early work, shows him to be a master draftsman. He acquired full control of the basics of painting—then followed his instincts.

The good instinctive manager does the same thing. One successful company president remarked, "I have learned management disciplines and I respect them—but I follow my instincts." He makes decisions that sometimes seem to come out of thin air. They do not. They result from powerful creative processes operating freely within a framework of discipline.

A manager is following a positive instinctive style when his instinct sometimes impels him toward distasteful decisions—and he makes them. An executive whose "instinct" always seems to point toward the more pleasant path is being self-indulgent. The chief executive who moves headquarters to California because he would like to live there is not going by a feel for what is important; he is just enjoying himself.

Instinctive management can lead to spectacular success, but only if it is grounded in the disciplines and the essentials of the business.

Management by Leadership

The leader is the executive who manages with wisdom, flair, and vision. He listens to his troops, prods them for information and ideas, and then leads them—with banners flying—into the arena of the marketplace.

This manager is sensitive to nuances. He keeps his antennae tuned to the feelings of subordinates, encouraging them to participate in discussions leading to corporate judgments. Even when a subordinate sees a decision go against him, he knows that he has had his chance to influence the course of events.

Leadership need not be the exclusive province of the chief executive. An enlightened CEO will do his best to inspire and cultivate leadership qualities in the key members of his team. He delegates, but he does not abdicate. This CEO sets up subleaders, who in turn become leaders within their own departments or divisions.

As Peter Drucker observes: "The executive . . . stimulates others to develop themselves, whether they are subordinates or colleagues. He sets standards which are not personal but grounded in the requirements of the task. At the same time, they are demands for excellence. For they are demands for high aspiration, for ambitious goals, and for work of great impact."

There is no one correct style. The genuine leader in management operates in a style that is really a constellation of the most effective elements of a number of styles. However, there are two characteristics of the most successful style. For one thing, it is *suited* to the manager who uses it. As we will see, style is not necessarily something the individual is born with and can do nothing to change. A manager can modify his style, but if the style he manifests is going to make him an effective leader, it can't be phony.

For example, take that elusive and misleading word "charisma." Some managers feel that the only way to succeed is by being charismatic—and to them this means being dashing and spectacular in all aspects of the job. But charisma is vastly overrated as a factor in managerial success. Its influence even becomes pernicious when an executive acts in a way that is totally alien to his nature because he thinks this is the way to be a leader.

A second hallmark of the leadership style is that it is *appropriate*. The style must not only suit the manager; it must fit the circumstances within which it operates—the type of business, the backgrounds and personalities of the people in that business, the nature of the industry. An executive may be a master of the instinctive approach, but if he moves into a company in which consensus management has been accepted as a way of corporate life, he is in trouble. His command of style may be complete, but he is using it in the wrong place.

Most successful styles contain elements of instinct and manipulation. The winning manager is sometimes a politician, sometimes a despot, sometimes a seeker of consensus. He listens, he prods for ideas, he plans. He is approachable, but he is not a pushover for a new proposal. He makes his subordinates work hard to sell him a proposition.

Successful managers come in all shapes and sizes and types of personality. Some are outgoing and friendly; others are introverted and taciturn. Some are even practically invisible. The invisible approach is a very hard one to bring off, but there are those who can make it work. But all successful managers have a sense of the importance of style. They have used their present styles with an eye on the realities.

As we proceed, we'll consider how the executive can diagnose his present style, evaluate it, and perfect a style that gets results.

3 -

Symptoms of a Defective Management Style

WHEN an executive's style is wrong for the job or the company, the difficulty may destroy not only the executive's effectiveness but the effectiveness of others around him as well.

Usually a manager's style is not totally defective. Problems arise when he moves to a new company, or into a new job, and the style that previously served him well no longer is right. There is then a mismatch. The individual whose management by instinct was nearly perfect for the sales manager's job, for instance, cannot get by with it anymore when he is promoted to vice president of marketing. The president who ruled his previous firm with an iron fist—and made this style work—takes over another company with a looser atmosphere and no longer can get results.

Two specific experiences with clients show how a particular style can be inappropriate for one job and highly effective for another. In the first case, a staff man was moved into a line job. He was made head of an operating division:

As a staff executive, this man didn't make decisions. His style was a combination of consensus and manipulation, a combination that fitted his needs very well. He was able to work indirectly to get results, and he was able to keep everybody happy.

Of course, the requirements of the line job were different. Now this man had to make decisions. He had to decide on major investments and determine where to spend and where to cut. He could not afford to be concerned with pleasing everyone.

The manager did not adapt. He continued to manage through manipulation and consensus. He relied too heavily on his department heads to make decisions that he should have been making. Performance declined. The chief executive of the company, looking over what was happening, commented, "The whole trouble is his style."

By contrast, in another company a successful manager was switched from line to staff. He had compiled a good record as a line man. He was considered a man who could get things done. The company's corporate planning operation needed to be straightened out, so this man was switched into it.

Management by inertia.

The style he had used to such good effect in the line job—a combination of leadership and despotism—didn't fit the new responsibility. People came to him for advice and counsel, and he gave them orders. The fact is that he knew more about what should be done than many of those who came to him, but that didn't matter. There was friction. Instead of getting straightened out, the staff operation deteriorated. The company probably should have switched this manager back into a line job, but there was no opening available and so they fired him.

There is always an interplay between management style and job.

Defects in style are relative to the situation in which the manager is placed. An executive may have vast resources of experience and skill, but if his style is not right for the job he—and the organization—will run into trouble. However—and this is a factor that exacerbates the problem of stylistic mismatch—it may be several years before the full measure of the difficulty shows up on the bottom line.

Some time ago the president of a manufacturing company was offered the job of chief executive of a firm in a different field. He had lunch with me and another friend who happened to head another company in the new field. We agreed that the man contemplating the move had all the equipment to handle the job. However, his style was one of quiet leadership. He would be replacing a CEO who had managed by means of noisy confusion. Our consensus was that it would take two to three years for the radically different style to show results.

It took every bit of that. In the end, the results

were good. But there were times when my friend did not think he could stick it out.

There are many occasions when the results are not so good. In one typical example, a corporation comprising three operating companies needed a new chief operating officer to take over one of the component firms. The chairman selected a man who had been executive vice president of a subsidiary:

Johnson, who had an accounting background, had shown himself to be adept at cutting costs. Furthermore, given an assignment in Washington, Johnson turned out to be remarkably skilled at dealing with politicians and getting government business.

Johnson gave many superficial indications of being a positive, creative leader. However, if his career had been examined more closely, it would have become evident that he was, at heart, a born manipulator. He told people what they wanted to hear and kept potentially strong subordinates off balance.

This management style, which may be right for a lot of situations, was wrong for the spot into which Johnson moved. But that fact did not become apparent until too late. After eighteen months, the performance of the key subsidiary fell off. Desperate efforts failed to shore it up. Johnson was replaced, but by that time the slippage had become a landslide and eventually the whole organization went into receivership.

It can be years before the negative effects of an inappropriate management style show up on the balance sheet. However, there are certain symptoms of defective style that can be perceived at an earlier stage. One of my first consulting assignments gave me an example of this when the chairman/chief executive of a client company asked me to see the newly appointed president. Let's call him Phil Erwin.

Erwin had been selected to provide strong leadership for an organization that was about to make a bid for market domination. He had a reputation for being a shrewd and resourceful manager and an excellent judge of talent.

Obviously, in our meeting, Erwin was supposed to be evaluating me. The meeting lasted two and a half hours with Erwin talking almost the entire time. I said yes and no and smiled. Later he told the chairman that I was the "smartest consultant" he had ever met.

This experience taught me a number of things. One of its effects was to make me wonder about Phil Erwin. I suspected that his management style was not the one of decisive leadership on which his reputation was based. This turned out to be true. Erwin proved to be anything *but* a good judge of men. He never listened enough. In the end his shortcomings in style led to disappointment and loss and he was replaced.

A real leader listens. He is not so absorbed in himself as to keep the other guy from talking. This trait of self-absorption is a matter of style. Its existence can provide early warning of problems in executive performance.

There are other symptoms of defective style that should flash a red alert to indicate that a manager may not be right for the job.

Rigidity

Styles can be modified, but not to the point of being phony. When a manager moves into a new company or a new job, he is likely to size up the situation and—if necessary—adapt his style, instinctively or deliberately.

Most new management situations require at least some degree of adaptation. When an executive displays rigidity, he may well be showing that he lacks the quality of adaptability that he needs to make adjustments required for good performance:

Harry Winslow had been second-in-command of a multipurpose company. One of his principal tasks had been to sit in on—and frequently conduct—meetings of division heads. The participants in these meetings discussed matters of broad company policy. The main purpose was to bring the sometimes divergent objectives and methods of the divisions into conformity with overall corporate goals.

Winslow was recruited to take over as president of another company. His new firm had many similarities with the previous one, but there was one important difference. This was a single-purpose company, manufacturing one line of products and marketing through one well-established distribution system.

The new president immediately instituted the practice of holding frequent meetings with key executives. This had not been the case before. The managers began to complain about the time spent in the meetings, preparing for the meetings, and dealing with the fallout from the meetings.

When Winslow's board chairman asked him about the usefulness of so many conferences, he replied by talking about how well the practice had worked in his previous company. Nothing was done; the meetings continued. Two years later it was obvious that the company's product and service were beginning to slip badly. It took another six months for Winslow to be replaced.

Harry Winslow was single-mindedly applying techniques that had been effective in a multipurpose company to the operation of a single-purpose company, where they were inappropriate. In the other firm the meetings had served a purpose. Furthermore, Winslow had come to depend on them. His basic approach to management was the consensus style.

It took a long time for Winslow's defective style to show up so markedly in performance that it became obvious something was seriously wrong. But the CEO might well have done some hard thinking when he first detected the symptom of rigidity in his new president.

Customer Dissatisfaction

Mergenthaler had come up through the creative side in a series of advertising agencies. As creative chief of a large agency, he had presided over the conception of some brilliant campaigns. The agency had always been heavily oriented toward client service, and all previous presidents had been account managers. But there was a new trend in advertising toward elevation of the creative function to the pinnacle; and so, when the president retired, Mergenthaler was given the job by majority vote.

Not all the members of the board were in favor. Some said that Mergenthaler, though undoubtedly brilliant, was not well rounded enough to handle the responsibility. They predicted that he would not get along well with the people with whom he had to get along.

His defenders pointed to the fact that Mergenthaler had attracted and held a formidable group of copywriters, art directors, and producers to the agency. "These are tough babies," one said. "If he can handle them, he can handle anybody."

As the new president took hold of his job, there were many promising signs. The creative division was given even greater strength, and this was reflected in a dazzling variety of advertising awards newly added to the cabinets in the reception room.

But there were certain rumblings. One board member heard from the top men in two client companies—one directly and one indirectly—that they were not happy. They could not pin it down, but they did not feel the agency's traditionally high degree of customer service was being maintained. Other board members reported hearing the same thing.

Mergenthaler dismissed all this as inconsequential. The advertising, he insisted, was what counted; and it was not only winning prizes, it was selling merchandise.

Everything seemed to go all right for a while. And then the roof fell in. The agency lost $45 million in billing within little more than a year. Under pressure, Mergenthaler resigned to start his own small "hot" creative agency.

Mergenthaler's style was perfectly adapted to working with difficult but brilliant creative people. But he was ineffective with the other branches of the company: media, research, and, in particular, account service. His insensitivity in this area had seriously hurt long-standing relationships and had driven old clients to seek new agencies.

The first indication of a defect in management style may be customer complaints. Even if there doesn't seem to be any sound basis to them at first, they can be the heralds of dire things to come.

Alienation of Subordinates

When an executive is given a job of high responsibility, it is emphatically not cricket to poll his subordinates about their opinions of him. Nevertheless, it is often possible to sense the feelings of the staff, and these feelings may indicate a symptom of defective style that will have serious consequences.

Floyd Cullinan had been a successful financial executive in the relatively relaxed atmosphere of the headquarters of Fielding & Company. He did not do much, but there was not much that had to be done. Fielding enjoyed the advantage of distinct product superiority, and so cost control—Cullinan's most direct responsibility—was not all that important.

Then Fielding acquired a subsidiary of quite a different nature and Cullinan was put in charge. Here cost control was extremely important. Although Cullinan was now faced with new responsibility, he maintained his natural style of invisibility.

He worked long hours, coming in early and leaving late, but he never could be found. He was inaccessible. Key managers were constantly asking each other, "Where is he?" This fact was quite evident to Fielding's top management people, but they ignored it until it was very late in the game. Cullinan took to locking his office door and never appearing. He finally suffered a nervous breakdown.

In another case of the invisible style, the efforts of employees to get in contact with the boss took a bizarre turn, but one which should have been significant to top management:

Geffkin had put together an enviable record as a marketing staff man, but like the unfortunate Cullinan, his style was that of invisibility. Then he was chosen to take over a manufacturing subsidiary.

Geffkin could not make decisions. He got scared. He stayed in his office overlooking the plant yard, stayed there so much, in fact, that frustrated employees actually took to throwing pebbles at the office window simply to try to attract his attention. The executive committee noted this display but wrote it off as another of the aberrations of employee behavior that had occasionally plagued the operation. But it was a symptom which should not have been ignored. Geffkin's inappropriate style made him ineffective as a manager and ultimately he had to be fired.

Extremity of Viewpoint

New brooms have a tendency to sweep. Every chief executive knows that. When a new manager comes on to a new and more important job, he wants to make changes. But the executive who wants to change *everything* may be displaying early symptoms of a mismatch in style that will destroy his ability to perform:

Roger Carmichael managed by creativity. His ideas were usually so acute and penetrating that his relative lack of effectiveness in executing plans through subordinates did not amount to a serious problem; at least, it was not serious in the series of jobs he had held as he made his way up through the organization.

Carmichael was given a new and more demanding post, in a different division. Within a week of taking over, he remarked to his president, "There isn't a single manager here who knows what he's doing. Everything's been handled wrong. I'm going to have to straighten the whole thing out from top to bottom."

The president made a mental note that this was a pretty extreme viewpoint. After all, not everything could be that bad. They must have been doing something right. But, in line with his commitment to give the newly appointed Carmichael a free hand, he said nothing.

Carmichael made an awesome number of changes in policy and personnel. And for a while things went rather well, propelled by the freshness and brilliance of Carmichael's creative mind. But then it all began to fall apart. Carmichael had gotten rid of some people who did have value. He was unable to get along with others. In his efforts to change everything he was introducing a new idea per week, and the structure could not handle all this change. The inevitable collapse led the president to reflect that he should have been warned by the extreme nature of Roger Carmichael's views as expressed when he took over. The president was right.

The man who takes over a new job cannot know everything there is to know, and he cannot change everything. Unwillingness or inability to admit these realities is a symptom of a management ailment that can become terminal.

Lack of Clear-Cut Assignments

Henry Bleek came to his new job at Belwether International with banners flying. He had stamped himself as a cyclone of activity in his previous assignments; and, while his efforts had not been crowned with the greatest successes, there seemed to be plenty of extenuating circumstances to indicate that this was not his fault.

Bleek had been on the job for three months when the Belwether chairman dropped in for one of his periodic visits. They fell to talking over the organizational changes that Bleek had indicated he was making. "What have you got Jeff Ryan doing?" asked the chairman.

The reply was somewhat vague. Bleek explained that Ryan was handling some special assignments in connection with a new plan that was, as yet, not fully spelled out. The chairman asked about another subordinate. This man's job was not described clearly either. When asked what a third manager was doing, Bleek gave an answer which seemed to indicate that this individual's duties somewhat overlapped those of the other two. The chairman was a little perplexed, but he consoled himself with the reminder that Bleek had a fine reputation and must know what he was doing.

Bleek had been considered a leader, but what he was demonstrating here were virulent symptoms of an extreme case of management by manipulation. The manipulative style is not necessarily bad. There are circumstances in which it can work quite well—but these circumstances did not apply here. Bleek had not been brought in to be a manipulator, yet that's what he was doing by keeping assignments vague and pitting one manager against another.

It was much, much later—after Bleek had clearly failed—that the chairman thought back and told himself that he might have been a little more attentive to this clue indicating a discordant style.

Proliferation of Staff

One prevailing indicator of the manager who cannot make decisions is the proliferation of jobs and layers of staff.

Andy Tyson had done well at every assignment he'd been given. These had all been subordinate assignments, but top management thought he was now ready to take on the general manager's job. Tyson was given a free hand.

His early results showed up most plainly on the organization chart. Tyson soon introduced two new tiers of supervision in the structure. He went even further in creating staff jobs. Within a short time he had staff people to advise on packaging, employee relations, fringe benefits, and transportation. He even hired a psychologist to evaluate people on the payroll as well as those applying for jobs.

Andy Tyson was a classic example of management by indecision. Faced with the need to act, he became extremely insecure. Instead of addressing himself to problems, he insulated himself against them by throwing up organizational barriers.

When a new manager seems to be going all out to add boxes to the chart and people to the payroll, he is exhibiting a symptom that should be looked into.

Arrogance

Tony Spiro was a very attractive man—not necessarily in looks, but in brains. He talked incessantly, but his monologues were so penetrating and so rich in flashing insights that he had a hypnotic effect on his listeners.

Glen Vale, chairman of the Deneb Corporation, felt lucky to get Spiro as president. But even Vale was astounded when Spiro announced, shortly after taking over, that he had worked out a plan that would give Deneb 200 percent growth within one year.

The chairman approached the president with some mild questions: Since there was no precedent in the industry for any company's making such a fantastic jump, was the projection not a little optimistic? Were the data on which Spiro based his forecast sound enough and extensive enough? Did Deneb possess the resources to fully carry out every aspect of the program? Would they not run serious risks of overextension in some areas if the plan failed to work in any of its interrelated aspects? And so forth.

Spiro was very touchy about being questioned in this fashion. His general attitude was, "If you don't like the way I'm handling it, get somebody else." He was unwilling to hedge on anything.

Vale was still uneasy, but he was persuaded by Spiro's

brilliance and his complete self-confidence. The Deneb Company plunged ahead—and soon was floundering in a morass.

It was not that Spiro's ideas weren't good. Most of them had considerable merit. But the whole scheme hinged on total success. When one element of the program started to fall short, the others were hurt. The situation deteriorated rapidly. Deneb was in trouble in terms of the profit picture, because volume was not commensurate with the expansion that Spiro had dictated. Furthermore, there was difficulty with the SEC; unfortunately the prospectus for potential investors had been based to a heavy extent on Spiro's dream.

Ultimately, Tony Spiro went into consulting work, where he is highly successful. His ideas don't have to be bought wholesale by clients. They are able to modify and trim them as they choose. As for Deneb, which survived—but just barely—the company is now getting along with a president whose visions are more modest but whose accomplishments are more substantial.

The manager who takes over a new assignment with a grandiose statement of what he is going to do is not necessarily wrong. But he should be willing—indeed, eager—to support his claims with data. When he acts as if the only opinion of any importance is his own, he is displaying the prime symptom of management by intellectual arrogance. He may be able to get away with it, but his own boss should be aware of the dangers that may lie ahead.

Excessive Need for Approval

Intellectual arrogance is one form of vanity. There is another form, in which the big thing is not self-approval but the need for the approval of others:

Harvey Arneson was a handsome man. In fact, he had done considerable modeling in his younger days and still was occasionally asked if he would like to do TV work. But Arneson was a successful and highly regarded marketing executive.

Some members of the board wondered about Arneson when he was made vice president of marketing. The division had been a hotbed of dissent, and they wondered if Arneson—with all of his grace and attractiveness—was really strong enough to enter the lions' den and quell its inhabitants.

However, Arneson's many supporters pointed out that he had more than looks. He got along with people, he was superb in a meeting, and he communicated ideas with such effectiveness as to make it look easy.

Harvey Arneson was not in the job for long when his top management began to feel good about things. There was a different atmosphere in marketing. For the first time in anyone's memory the division seemed to be in harmony. The backbiting and complaints appeared to have dropped off to a trickle.

There was just one thing wrong. The marketing division was not accomplishing much. Harvey Arneson's style was to keep everybody happy. He made promises, he approved pet ideas, he stroked people. The hubbub subsided, but so did the creative output.

When a manager takes over an operation and suddenly everyone's spirits pick up, the situation may not be as good as it looks. The surface bliss may conceal some very troublesome realities. Unusual harmony—like unusual bitterness—can be an important symptom of a harmful stylistic imbalance.

We have reviewed some of the major symptoms of defective style. No single indication may be conclusive in itself. But such clues may well signal trouble—caused by a mismatch in style—before it becomes critical.

4 –

Style in Planning and Decision Making

STYLE has a distinct influence on decision making and planning. The methods of making executive decisions vary widely, but all managers go through certain essential steps. The manager must first be sure what he is deciding about. He makes himself aware of the problems and the opportunities. He also determines whether it is a one-shot decision or one that will recur regularly. This determination influences his thinking about the kind of policy that should be developed.

Is there a current plan that is supposed to apply to the situation? If there is, then the plan may have to be modified. If there is no plan, one will have to be developed.

The manager sets his objectives and comes to a tentative determination of the broad strategy needed to attain the objectives. He thinks about the implications of the strategy in terms of money, organization, and people. The strategy is reassessed in the light of these considerations.

At this point a set of tactics is developed. The manager projects the implementation of these tactics into the future. He tries to anticipate the complex of actions and interactions that will be set in motion once the decision is made. The tactics themselves are assessed and reassessed, alternatives are considered, and finally the decision is made.

In major decisions these steps will be gone through formally. The executive also makes everyday decisions of smaller scope. Here he may not go through a formal step-by-step procedure; he just goes ahead and decides. But usually he has not ignored the primary requirements of the decision-making process; he has "telescoped" them, incorporating them into a more informal process.

Management style has an important bearing on the making of decisions, large and small. Take the case of a consumer products company which I'll call Fabulous Inc.

For years Fabulous had enjoyed a leading market share with one of its products. The product was a superior one, and Fabulous knew how to sell it.

The situation began to change when the principal competitor in the field achieved a product breakthrough. The competitor began to take his product market-by-market in a strong bid to cut into the lead Fabulous had held for so long.

The tactics were working. Fabulous's market share started to decline. The various members of the top management team reacted in accordance with their styles.

The marketing vice president, John Denton, managed by creativity and manipulation. He tended to go for the bold, sweeping move rather than to play it safe. One of his biggest failings was an inclination to skimp on research and play hunches.

Denton was not only concerned about the slippage; he was angry about it. The marketing vice president liked being number one, and he wanted to stay that way. His instinctive reaction was to push for an all-out marketing effort to offset competition.

The company's financial vice president possessed a style of intellectual arrogance. He felt that he knew more than anyone else, not just about money, and he didn't mind letting it be known. This manager, George Gallagher, predicted sardonically that the decline in share would steepen, and that nothing would be done about it until too late. He disagreed with Denton about a big marketing push being the answer. Gallagher felt that Fabulous should significantly improve its product to strengthen its position.

Harry Clay, the president, managed by indecision. He hated to make up his mind about anything but the most pragmatic matter. If he could be shown that a course of action offered a distinct cost reduction, he would go for it. Otherwise, he would procrastinate.

Clay conceded that the company was losing market share, but he pointed out that there were advantages in sticking to the same product. The firm had made good strides in refining manufacturing methods and had been able to cut costs, so that

Management by rejection.

the profit picture was holding up. "Let's wait and see," he said. "We'll probably be all right."

The chairman, Lon Feiffer, was a consensus manager. He kept sending his key people back to the conference table, asking them to agree on a proposal.

Denton, the marketing man, put together a scheme for intensified advertising and beefed-up selling. The ad campaign would increase the use of TV, the company's principal vehicle, but would also move more heavily into print.

This marketing plan received no support from Gallagher, the financial vice president, and without his help, Denton was unable to win the president over.

Then the marketing and financial managers got together to make a joint plan. They came up with a two-pronged idea. The product would be redesigned, and new ways would be tested for marketing it. They went to the president with their proposition.

"This will cost ten million before we can even tell if it's working," said Clay. He opposed the move, and continued to oppose it. Meetings of the top four were a series of disputes. The CEO, Feiffer, seeing that a consensus had not been arrived at, stayed out of it.

Then Clay left on a two-week trip overseas. This was the chance Denton and Gallagher had been waiting for. They arranged to meet with Feiffer and presented their ideas in detail. For the first time they were able to tell their story the way they wanted to tell it, without Clay's opposition and negative interruptions. Furthermore, since the marketing and financial executives were familiar with the chairman's fondness for consensus, they showed that practically everyone in the organization was on their side except the president.

The chairman decided to approve the new plan and to persuade the president that it was the best course. When Clay came back, he was not hard to persuade. He did not like to take action himself, but when others took the responsibility for action, he was inclined to go along.

The moves were made; they worked. Fabulous was able to reverse the slump in its fortunes.

If any of the four people involved in this decision had managed by means of a true leadership style, the decision would have been made much earlier. The form and the timing of the decision were shaped by the styles of the managers who participated in making it.

In our next example, there are three protagonists. Paul Lewis, the chief executive officer of the company in question, manages by leadership and intuition. The president of the company, Elliot Meehan, has always leaned toward the inactive style. Tom Farr, the marketing vice president, is essentially a creative manager.

Lewis found himself in the pleasant and relatively rare position of having, for the moment, no really major problems to confront. Instead of coasting, he set out to look for the greatest opportunity for constructive effort over the next few years. The financial basis of the firm was sound. Costs were under good control. After some deliberation, Lewis concluded that the area offering the most room for improvement was marketing.

The CEO confided his opinion to Meehan, the president. Meehan conceded that there might be something in the idea; but, in a way that is typical of the inactive style, he said, "Let's make a study in depth of the situation."

Lewis knew his president. He knew that Meehan had many fine qualities. He was well liked in the company and in the industry, and, when impelled to action, he possessed valuable skill at reconciling opposing points of view and applying patient and painstaking administration to move a project through to completion.

But first the president had to be brought to the point at which he would be willing to act. The CEO did not want a broad, general study; that course offered too many excuses for delay and inaction. Instead, Lewis suggested a more sharply focused study of one particular product line, the "500" line.

Meehan wanted to know why they should concentrate on the "500" line immediately. After all, he protested, wouldn't that mean proceeding on an assumption? That is exactly what it *would* mean, but the CEO was unwilling to back off his assumption. He *knew* that there was considerable room for improvement in the "500" line, and that a study of the area would provide the facts that would convince Meehan.

The preliminary results of the study indicated that there were, indeed, problems with the chosen line. The marketing approach was not consistent. The difficulty of sale was greater than in other lines. As the analysis probed deeper, it became clear that the marketing group involved in selling the "500" line was lacking in dedication. Moreover, there was a lot of confusion in even the most routine operations. Within the group, it was dog eat dog.

By now Meehan, the president, could see that there was a problem in this area, but he wanted specifics. The study, designed by the CEO, unearthed the specifics: Within the group, the salary level was relatively low, the research effort was weak, there was no consistent marketing plan, morale was deficient. The group members felt they lacked proper access to the marketing vice president. They received no regular performance reviews, and they were skeptical about their chances for promotion.

As all this came out, Farr, the marketing vice president, was at first defensive. He was typical of those who manage by creativity: brilliant in innovation, but a lackluster administrator.

Little by little Farr began to realize that his own success lay in improved performance. He agreed that positive steps should be taken to improve the marketing of the "500" line. Meehan, the president, went along—although he continued to talk wistfully about the need for more study. Having won this much acceptance, the CEO said, "Let's not wait another minute: Let's go!" A plan was devised and implemented.

The styles of these managers shaped the way the decision came into being. Left to himself, the president would not have acted until things had gotten a lot worse. The marketing vice president would have realized the existence of the problem and might eventually have localized its source, but his defensiveness and lack of administrative ability make it doubtful that his solution would have been the most effective one.

The chief executive officer showed true leadership style. He saw, intuitively, the combination of problem and opportunity. He pitched in immediately to do something about it, at the same time bringing his colleagues along with him to ensure their willing participation in the implementation of the plan.

Decisions are a function of planning. Most organizations use two basic types of plan. There is a strategic corporate plan and an annual tactical plan developed by each of the major divisions of the company. The interaction of these plans can sometimes create areas of great difficulty, affecting decision making across the board.

Typically, the corporate planner projects the long-term outlook for the organization as a whole. His work becomes less specific as he moves outward from the present moment. For the year ahead, the corporate planner will come up with fairly precise projections; for the next year there will be fewer specifics, and so forth. In his work the corporate planner takes a broad look at the marketplace. He may use models or other means of accumulating and sorting out information.

The corporate planner arrives at tentative long-range goals, subject to the approval of top management. Then the long-range plan is given to the people who do the annual planning. These are line managers, who must come up with specific plans in such areas as marketing, finances, and manufacturing.

The annual planner performs a "bottoms up" analysis. He prices out the varying factors. He asks, "What will the market be? . . . What will the competition do? . . . If we take a certain action, what consequences will it have?"

The annual plan is reconciled with the strategic plan, with top management making the final decision in areas of conflict. The annual plan must then be translated into a technical plan, complete with financial data. At this stage the planners may have to go back over some or all of the preceding steps.

This is a typical picture of the kind of planning that is done by most large companies. Management style can have an enormous influence on the form and the effectiveness of the process.

I have seen corporate planners approach their task with such rigidly preconceived ideas about goals that they placed severe limitations on the options open to the financial planner. One corporate planner, whose style was management by despotism, would not even look objectively at research figures. Presented with a projection of 15 percent market growth, he would say, in effect, "I don't care what your reading of the potential is. We will not invest in this. Therefore, I say the market will not grow 15 percent; it will grow only 4 percent."

I have also observed corporate planners—particularly those who operated via the creative style—who were far too optimistic in their projections, placing an intolerable burden on the line managers who had to inflate their divisional goals to conform with the overly expansive long-range plan.

The operating manager of a division may see that such broad-scale optimism is unrealistic. He knows the market situation and the capabilities of his competitors better than the corporate planner does. But the line manager may fear to express his doubts. He doesn't want to be thought timid or negative, so he will go along with the grandiose projections and try to figure out some way to get the resources to meet them.

As an organization changes, so does the nature of the decisions affecting that organization. An executive whose decision-making style is appropriate for the growth stage may find that the same style renders him unable to make good decisions once the organization has reached maturity:

Randolph Hecker was a creative manager. He took over a new department with a new product and untested methods of production. Hecker's creative approach enabled him to make a lot of sound decisions right at the start. He made some mistakes, too, but the important thing was to generate enthusiasm and action.

But as the operation grew, Hecker's style lagged. He failed to adapt it to the altered circumstances. By now there were precedents; there was a need for order. And there was a growing body of data and experience that needed to be incorporated into the decision-making process.

Hecker continued to be guided by his hunches. He issued conflicting orders. He made random assignments. The result was confusion sometimes amounting to chaos. Many of his key people left. Those who stayed began to insist more emphatically that some order be imposed on the department, and that the decisions affecting their work be made with greater coherence and relevance.

One day Hecker was discussing the situation with two of his subordinates. One, an extremely methodical person, suggested that an elaborate procedure be set up to amass information and construct a set of policies that would govern all decisions, big and little. The other subordinate, an intuitive manager, declared that this would take too long. He had a proposal that should be put into play immediately. However, he had no facts to back it up.

The president of the company, Ben Shaw, walked in and stood listening to the discussion. Shaw knew what had to be done, but he had to present his ideas in such a way that they would not be offensive. He could see that if nothing were done, Hecker would go off on a tangent without getting to the heart of the matter.

Shaw listened. Then he said, "Everything you guys are saying makes sense. Let me see if I can—as a third party—phrase it so that it makes sense to you." After a few minutes the president offered a simple proposal involving no change in the substance of decisions, but a clear-cut way of setting up assignments. Shaw presented this as an idea that embodied the varying views of all of the others, but that was not quite the case. The idea was the president's alone, packaged to make it palatable.

Shaw was, for the moment, playing the role of a consensus manager. In reality his style was one of leadership. The exceptional leader acquires a mastery of the superficial appearances of other styles, because sometimes the temporary adoption of those superficial appearances is the best way for him to exert his leadership.

If Shaw had really been a consensus manager, he would have listened exhaustively to all the viewpoints and then tried to "average" them. If his style were that of indecision, he would have welcomed the disagreement and fostered it, because this would have deferred the necessity to act. As a leader, he not only knew what to do, he expressed assurance in a way that won support from his subordinates.

Effective planning requires more than experience and information. The man who does the planning should have a style that suits the task. The despot is not a good corporate planner; nor is the executive who manages by creativity. The best planners are much more likely to be those who manage by consensus and by detail.

Management style has a pervasive influence on decision making. The astute manager will examine the kinds of decisions that go with a job and see if the style of the man in the job matches up with them.

5 -

Management Style in Action: Five Case Histories

CORPORATE leaders are becoming increasingly aware of the vital role that style plays in the conduct of a business. Today it is commonplace to hear top managers say, "His style doesn't fit" or "We need a person with a different style."

The crux of the situation lies in the match-up between management style and job requirements.

An executive whose style is successful in one situation may be unable to perform well when he is moved into a different situation. An organization that is failing under one kind of management style turns around when it is taken over by an executive with a different approach.

Here are five case histories that demonstrate how managers with varying styles handle the same situation.

The Good News Pipe Company

The name of the company is not descriptive of its scope. Good News made and sold five product lines. A separate division was responsible for each. At the time of our story, one division was extremely profitable, another was marginally profitable, and three were operating at a loss.

Overall, Good News was making a small profit, but the stockholders were becoming dissatisfied with what they considered to be lagging performance.

The president of the company was Fred Bland, a personable executive and an exponent of the consensus style. He maintained a small central staff, including a personnel manager and a weak financial manager, and gave considerable scope to his division heads. Bland held frequent meetings with these managers, usually calling them together as a group. (Only rarely did he deal with his managers on a one-to-one basis.) At these group meetings, the president would ask his executives for their thoughts on how to increase profitability. The division managers were quite free with suggestions for the improvement of performance.

The trouble was that these suggestions were usually directed toward the improvement of *other* divisions—not the division being run by the manager making the recommendation. All the managers, including the one running the highly profitable division, took part in these verbal exercises.

Little if anything came out of the meetings. For one thing, because the divisional executives were almost always talking about someone else's problem, their remarks were deficient in precise knowledge or realistic solutions. And, since Bland was personally responsible for the investment in the losing divisions, he was hampered by an innate reluctance to admit error.

The manager of the most profitable line concentrated on promoting his own plan. Surveys had shown that the line would do well in foreign markets, and the executive in charge was anxious to receive a green light to expand overseas. However, Bland's practice of continually submitting this proposition for the consideration of the other managers put a damper on any real action.

The manager of the marginal division had taken steps to improve the product line so that it was now competitive with the leader in the field. But costly marketing and production methods had not been changed, and so the margin remained low.

The managers who were running the three losing operations devoted themselves to defenses of their own performance and promises that, "given time," they would show results.

At this point the board of directors decided to make a change. The chairman, Will Kaiser, declared that he would take over as chief executive officer. This was unacceptable to Fred Bland, and he soon left.

Kaiser was a despot, although an intelligent one. He did not move precipitately. He met with each division head separately. He quietly studied each product line—its position in the market, its competition, its opportunities for profit, its prospects for profit, its prospects for improvement. At the same time Kaiser addressed himself to certain problems at corporate headquarters. He found, for example, that Good News was consistently forecasting larger sales than were actually made, and budgeting its manpower accordingly. Kaiser concluded that a far more scientific approach was called for.

Having made his deliberations, Kaiser called in the top management team and said, "Here's what we are going to do." As the managers listened in astonishment, Kaiser outlined sweeping changes.

First, Good News would dispose of the three unprofitable divisions. The head of each division was made responsible for the liquidation of his own operation, with the process to start immediately.

Kaiser announced that the most profitable division would expand into foreign markets. The manager of this division smiled broadly at this welcome news, but the breadth of his smile lessened perceptibly when Kaiser went on to say, "I will make the decisions on how this is to be done."

As for the marginally profitable division, it would remain in business—but its performance would have to improve. One means of bringing this about was the retention of a consulting firm which would, as Kaiser put it, "tell us where to lop off heads."

Having delivered this message to his executives, Kaiser encouraged only the briefest period of comment before adjourning the meeting.

The course of action that Kaiser had outlined was, with certain possible exceptions, a sound one. Nevertheless, it got nowhere.

The managers of the profitable divisions, resentful of what they considered to be arbitrary and cavalier treatment, dragged their feet. The consulting firm made drastic recommendations for manpower cuts. They were accepted sullenly by management and implemented without much regard to quality or continuity. As for the managers of the losers, it is perhaps unsurprising that they found innumerable reasons to delay the consummation of their own suicides.

Seeing that Good News was still in trouble, the board acted again. Kaiser was persuaded to withdraw as chief executive. A new president, Jim Wynn, was brought in. Finally, the Good News Pipe Company had at its helm a possessor of a true leadership style.

Wynn did not make any sudden moves. He investigated and became thoroughly familiar with people, policies, and procedures. He talked with each division separately, asking them for counsel and information. When he felt he was on firm ground, he summoned the team together and talked about his plans.

To the manager of the most profitable division Wynn had this to say: "Joe, I agree with my predecessor that we should expand into international operations. I leave it up to *you* to determine how this can best be done, considering risks, estimate of return, and other pertinent factors. You have my go-ahead."

To the manager of the marginally profitable operation Wynn's message was: "Ted, you have indicated that we should make some changes, particularly in the marketing setup. Since we've been giving certain privileged customers special treatment, this involves some risk, but I'm willing to take the risk if you are. Let's develop a program to improve our marketing."

Then Wynn turned to the heads of the unprofitable divisions: "I'm sorry, but your lines are areas in which I can't see any future for the company. You've been asked to get rid of your own divisions. I think it's too much to require you to run them and sell them at the same time.

"You are all good men. We have growth plans, and we'll do our best to find places for you that are worthy of your talents. I think you will find the suggestions I am going to make will be more than satisfactory. If not, then you can be sure that we'll give you a most acceptable deal on severance and time.

"As for the disposition of the divisions, I will ask

an outside company—one that specializes in these matters—to handle the situation. If they don't come up with suitable answers in a reasonable time, we'll close the divisions down rather than permit them to continue to drain away money and energy."

Wynn then spoke to his financial chief, saying, "We agree that significant possible improvements can be made in our forecasting and budgeting. I'd like to bring in a consultant who can help us do this. Although I'd like to make the final approval, you will handle the arrangements."

The new president established timetables. He followed up by working with the individual executives. And, as a result of this application of the leadership style, Good News achieved a remarkable turnaround in performance.

Universal Equipment

This company had enjoyed a long and successful history. It had always prided itself on setting the standard for the industry. However, in recent years its industrial product line had become obsolescent in many important respects. Management methods and production capabilities had declined. New plants, equipment, and approaches were needed. The company's financial position was still reasonably good, but the curve had been declining for years.

Chet Doolittle had been the CEO at Universal for more than a decade. When he took over, the company had had modern plants and machines and a vigorous marketing approach. Doolittle was well liked and was able to keep things together, but essentially his management style was that of inaction. His principal aim was to maintain the status quo. His marketing people urged new and improved products and more aggressive selling methods. Their recommendations were deferred. Division heads proposed modernization of procedures and replacement of aging machines. They were told, "Let's think about it." The research department developed new products. They were not test-marketed. Doolittle's ultimate answer to everything was, "We've been doing all right, why change?" Meanwhile, competition was creeping up on and, in some cases, overtaking Universal.

The president—a well-liked person with the knack of making all of his pronouncements seem profound even when they were flimsy—was never in serious jeopardy of being ousted. However, the board of directors was not altogether unhappy when it came time for Doolittle to retire.

His chosen successor was Jeb Faust, an executive with some impressive credentials, but one whose creative style incorporated liberal doses of confusion. Faust had put together several small and dynamic businesses, moving on when the gestation process was complete. On the whole these enterprises had not panned out as profitably as had been hoped; nevertheless, Faust looked very good on paper.

The new president came in loaded with ideas. He encouraged each member of top management to offer ideas for improvement. Faust then proceeded to elaborate on these recommendations and add grandiose touches of his own. Managers went away dazzled, feeling that they had an open field to take vigorous and innovative action.

Curiously, though, all this scintillating activity produced few concrete results. Faust sincerely wanted to put a lot of plans into motion, but there was always something lacking in his ability to bring it off. He continued as the head of Universal for three years, to the deepening gloom of the directors, but then left to take a high-ranking government job.

Faust's replacement, Hector Cubbage, was a quite different type of executive. He was quiet and methodical; he managed by the numbers. Cubbage started by doing what Faust had done only sketchily; he took the time to make a painstaking study of each line—its profitability, competition, product, market share, need for innovation, and so on down the line.

Cubbage consulted each division head and staff member. These meetings were not the flights of fancy that had taken place under the aegis of Faust. The new president required action plans supported by full financial, research, and other pertinent data. He didn't inspire the troops, but he did challenge them to prove that their recommendations would produce acceptable results. This was in many ways a tiresome procedure. However, the managers found that once Cubbage was convinced of the correctness of the course, they were able to set in motion plans that made sense.

Under the management of Hector Cubbage, Universal has begun a slow but definite climb back to the top. There is one drawback in Cubbage's method; the time it takes him to decide on a new product or new marketing plan sometimes gives competition an edge—but on the whole Cubbage's style is producing far better results than did those of his two predecessors.

Dorchester Industries

Clive Rains had a good record as a division chief for Dorchester. His division competed successfully in a tough industrial market.

Rains' daily routine varied little. He came in promptly at 9 A.M., sometimes through the plant, sometimes through the reception area. He seldom spoke to anyone as he walked to his office. Once there, Rains closed his door, shutting off the noise and bustle of the traffic in the busy corridor. For the most part his door would remain closed throughout the day.

The division head placed complete confidence in three carefully chosen members. He would call each of them in separately to discuss activities in the manager's particular area. During these talks Rains would probe in considerable depth into areas that many executives stay away from—the personalities of subordinates, their problems, how they could be motivated, and similar matters. Every now and then Rains met with all three key managers as a group, but this was rare. On the whole, he laid out courses of action, kept track of things through progress reports, and gave his top people a great deal of autonomy.

Rains was not popular with the office and plant staff, but he was not unpopular either. They almost never saw him, so they had no feeling about him. Rains was a prime example of the invisible style.

This style enabled Clive Rains to enjoy considerable free time. Some days he didn't come in at all. On the whole, his absences were rarely noted.

Divisional results continued to be generally good. This success rested largely on the strength of Rains' strong and loyal key subordinates. Also, Rains possessed well-developed instincts which helped him to sense problems and straighten them out, even though he remained aloof from the arena.

However, clouds were gathering. There were changes in the top management echelons at Dorchester, and certain members of the newly constituted team were unhappy with Rains' occasional unavailability and his seeming unfriendliness. They approached him in a series of moves designed to try to correct what they saw as his shortcomings.

Now Clive Rains, though his on-the-job conduct could not have been more quiet, was not without a temper. In fact, one of the reasons that Rains had adopted an invisible style was his tendency to fly off the handle when confronted with attitudes or activities of which he disapproved. He bridled at the comments of his superiors. He pointed, reasonably enough, to his record of success. And finally, in a climactic meeting at headquarters, Rains blew his top and told his bosses what he thought of them.

Rains was fired.

The replacement chosen by the Dorchester top brass was a man who—on the surface—could not have been more different from Rains. Charley Goodfellow had a flamboyant, outgoing personality. He spent a lot of time walking around the plant and office, chatting with people ("How's the family, Jack? How's it going, Maude?"). He was able to project an air of concern for the well-being of everyone he met.

Superficially Goodfellow manifested a blend of styles—leadership, creativity, manipulation. But the facade was very misleading. Underneath all this, Charley Goodfellow was a true despot. His apparent easy-going benevolence was a cloak for a cold, calculating drive to dominate people and destroy them. He smiled with his mouth, but never with his eyes.

Goodfellow fired the three senior executives upon whom Rains had relied, suspecting them of continuing loyalty to the departed division chief. He brought in assistants who were little more than toadies. His manner of issuing orders was pleasant, but employees came to realize that whether they agreed or not, they must follow instructions to the letter or be castigated and, perhaps, discharged. Many of the actions that Goodfellow set in motion were wrong to begin with. Others had merit, but won little real cooperation from the staff, who had by now labeled Goodfellow as a phony.

Charley Goodfellow lasted two years as the head of the division. During his second year it started to go downhill rapidly, and Dorchester got rid of him. An attempt was made to lure Clive Rains back to the job, but he refused.

They still are looking.

Wagstaff Inc.

Wagstaff is a medium-size service company which for many years was highly regarded for its energetic and innovative management.

One of the outstanding members of the Wagstaff team was Lee Starr, the marketing director. Starr's style was instinctive, with a strong dash of creativity. He maintained a small staff, and kept his people charged up with inspiration. Starr's operation was a beehive of new approaches, interesting ideas, bold marketing departures, and far-reaching plans.

Not all of these notions got off the drawing board, but those that were put into operation were, on the whole, remarkably successful. The counterbalance to Starr's ingenuity was provided by the general manager, Aaron Dimsworth.

Dimsworth was an executive quite different from Starr. He was a true representative of the methodical style. He evaluated each of Starr's marketing proposals carefully, costing them out to an intense degree. Sometimes the marketing head and his staff became impatient with Dimsworth's meticulous approach, but Starr kept a rein on this impatience, in part because he sensed that Dimsworth was screening out proposals that probably wouldn't work, and also because Dimsworth's cooperation was invaluable in implementing even the best of schemes. The relationship between two managers of markedly different styles was working out quite well.

Eventually the president of Wagstaff announced his plan to retire. The board, without much dissent, bestowed the job on Lee Starr.

Starr moved behind the president's desk with great optimism. His accession was accompanied by a flurry of innovative activity as he continued to produce brilliant ideas.

Before long it became apparent that something was wrong. Many of Starr's ideas that were put into operation didn't pan out as well as his track record warranted. A lot of other plans bounced around the executive suite for a long time without ever being implemented. The trouble was not that Starr had changed his style; he was as instinctive and creative as ever. But now he had lost his balance wheel. Dimsworth was no longer subjecting Starr's flashes of insight to methodical analysis. Moreover, Starr now had the responsibility for arranging implementation, and follow-through was not his long suit.

Wagstaff is experiencing difficulties, and the board of directors is wondering what to do about it.

Ariel Chemicals

On the whole, Ariel Chemicals seemed to have few major problems. It manufactured and marketed products in three areas. One, the "A" line, was recognized as the leader in its field. Ariel's "A" line had long since outstripped its competitors. The product's superiority was by now accepted as a standard in the industry. Since competition was not keen, little innovative effort was required to keep margins at a comfortable level.

The "B" line did not enjoy quite as happy a situation, but it was doing all right. This line was marketed in a keenly competitive area. However, the "B" line had—through constant improvement and strenuous selling—maintained a good profit picture. Given the toughness of the market, it didn't appear realistic to mount real growth plans for the "B" line, but the board didn't lose any sleep over the situation.

The reef beneath the surface of the peaceful lagoon was the "C" line. These products required constant innovation—plus heavy advertising, merchandising, and packaging support—to even survive against shark-like competition. Even so, this area of the business was operating at a rather large loss. The fact that the other two lines more than made up for the deficit was of short-term consolation, but the problem remained.

The president of Ariel at this time was John Swift. Swift was noted in the industry for his sharp tongue, his incisive mind, and the biting sarcasm with which he responded to any questioning of his stewardship. Swift knew the company and the industry. Many of his moves were extremely sound. He exhibited a lot of the attributes of leadership, but his style was actually that of intellectual arrogance.

Swift was largely responsible for the institution of the "C" line, and he was scornful of those who had reservations about its eventual success. He had little respect for the intelligence of any member of the board of directors—or, at least, so they were led to think. He made moves without even a pretense of taking them into his confidence. And he stubbornly resisted suggestions that something be done about the unprofitable "C" line, while he wouldn't even listen to proposals that changes might be needed in the struggling "B" line.

At last the board became fed up with Swift's arrogance and lack of responsiveness and decided on a successor.

The new president of Ariel was Manfred Chessman. Chessman had acquired a good reputation as top man in a couple of other companies. His style was that of a skilled manipulator. He tended to appoint managers of exceedingly modest abilities to important jobs and play them off against each other. Nor did his manipulative predilections confine themselves to people; he was not above a touch of financial manipulation as well.

Following form, Chessman made changes, placing weak executives in key posts. He appointed one puppet to head the "C" division, having assured the board that this was the very person needed to shore up this vulnerable spot. When nothing happened, Chessman declared himself to be disappointed and chose another feeble replacement. His reign produced a lot of manipulative activity with few positive results.

The board caught on to the lack of real progress and made another change. This time they were fortunate enough to select a strong leader.

Management by manipulation.

The new president of Ariel, Philip Paladine, seasoned his leadership style with intuition. His quick study of the company's situation convinced him that things were worse than they had appeared. Ariel was still showing a profit, but strong measures were necessary to prevent the firm from lapsing into a marked decline.

Paladine came to some far-reaching decisions. Previously there had been little emphasis on the "A" division, since this line was showing a good profit. Paladine did not agree; he decided to capitalize on the innate strength of the line to build the margin even more. The executive at the head of this unit was a good man, but Paladine impressed on him the necessity of careful innovation that would exploit the "A" line's leadership position. Paladine proposed to make available to the "A" division resources that would give new life to its technical and merchandising efforts.

As for the "B" line, Paladine concluded that this was an area from which Ariel could derive profit for some time to come, but within which there was little potential. So he conferred with the division head to establish guidelines for innovative marketing activity. Ariel would continue to pour resources into the "B" line to try to push its market share up a few points against fierce and well-established competition.

Paladine had at first thought that he would discontinue the unprofitable "C" line but, as he examined the situation, he sensed that there were possibilities there. Swift had not been altogether misguided in instituting this line; but his unwillingness to listen to suggestions had hurt its performance. Under the manipulative Chessman the "C" line had continued to languish because there was no strong leadership to give it a thrust.

The new president decided to give "C" division a run for its money once and for all. He talked with the man running the division, assured him that a place would be found for him in the organization, but said that he was bringing in a strong young executive to take over. Paladine had already recruited this man and assured him that he would receive the support necessary to turn "C" division around if it could be done.

At this point Paladine called the division chiefs together, informed them of his plans for the unprofitable line, and asked their counsel on how the other divisions could be improved. He talked with Ariel's financial officer about the realities of the considerable investment needed to exploit the "A" line's leadership and turn the "C" line into a profit maker. He prepared a five-year forecast and took the board into his confidence, laying out the unpalatable facts about necessary investment along with the risks and chances for success.

The board realized that for the next year or two there would be a considerable diminution of profit as Paladine made his moves. They concluded that Paladine was a leader worth investing in, and they agreed to the course he proposed. On the whole the executives of the company agreed that the new president knew what he was doing and was embarked on the best possible course.

Ariel is now in the third year of Paladine's plan.

The first two years were rough; but now the profit picture has improved greatly, and the company is healthier than it has been for many years.

A manager's style is not necessarily good or bad by itself. It is only in the style's match-up with the job that its worth is proved. Executive performance depends, to a considerable degree, on the solid linkage of style to circumstances and to the requirements of the management task.

What's Your Style?

At this point you may well have a pretty good idea of your own style. To get the most out of the rest of this book, it's a good idea to know the style—or mixture of styles—that dominates your management approach.

As a review, look over this checklist of the major criteria that identify each of the styles we have discussed. Clues to style lie in the executive's feelings and practices in relating to people (one-on-one or in groups), communicating, reacting to ideas, and approaching decisions. Here are some guidelines.

The inactive style

- The inactive manager is always willing to let a decision go one more day.
- When something goes wrong, he assumes that hasty action is the likely cause.
- He is uneasy with colleagues and subordinates who push hard.

- His idea of a smooth-running operation is one that needs little guidance.
- He prefers discussion meetings to meetings that require decisions.

The detail style

- This manager enjoys reading detailed material and amassing minute pieces of data.
- He maintains and uses voluminous files.
- When confronted with a decision, he looks for more facts.
- He does not feel comfortable with instinctive people.
- When something goes wrong, he is prone to assume that the problem stems from lack of adequate information.
- He likes meeting with definite agendas, at which people contribute facts.

The invisible style

- The invisible manager relies on information and a few trusted associates.
- He prefers to work alone.
- He avoids meetings to the extent that he can.
- His communication is largely via the written word.
- He considers small talk and socializing a waste of time.
- When interrupted, he is impatient to return to his solitary labors.

The manipulative style

- The manipulator is proud of his ability to get people to do what he wishes.
- He sees his staff in terms of how they balance off and rival one another.
- He makes up his mind first, then maneuvers people into line.

- When a subordinate disagrees with him, he concentrates on winning agreement to the exclusion of almost everything else.
- At meetings, the manipulator tries to control the proceedings while giving the appearance of free-ranging discussion.

The rejection style
- The rejector invariably looks for the negative side of any proposal.
- He mistrusts optimists.
- He does not worry about missing opportunities through lack of bold action. His risks are negative risks.
- At meetings he is a "counterpuncher," tending to criticize ideas.
- He solemnly and eloquently defends the status quo.

The survival style
- The survivor tends to avoid risks.
- He is willing to delegate, if it does not entail too much risk.
- Confronted with a decision, he tries to determine the safest course for him.
- He is uncomfortable with strong subordinates.
- At meetings he confines his participation to looking good rather than making a contribution.

The despotic style
- Goals are all-important to the despot; the means of reaching them is secondary.
- He is basically contemptuous of colleagues and subordinates.
- He does not delegate.
- He is willing to take risks on his own judgment.

- He is ruthless with people.
- His meetings are rigidly controlled.

The creative style
- The creative manager likes to sit and think about many aspects of the business.
- He values unusual and imaginative people.
- He is impatient with a heavy diet of detail.
- Free-wheeling discussion marks the meetings that he runs; he is more an equal participant than a leader.
- When things go along without too much action he becomes uneasy.
- In dealing with people he prods for more imaginative solutions and different angles.

The leadership style
- The leader values people primarily for their talent and contribution.
- He is not afraid to take a new position and make it attractive.
- People respect him and respond to him.
- He enjoys dealing with people face to face.
- He is equally comfortable with workers at all levels of the organization.
- He will intervene at meetings to push for the best possible solution; but he will not try to dominate the discussion.
- He is self-confident, but he steps back and evaluates himself from time to time.

These criteria—and others that will occur to you—will provide you with the objectivity to see yourself as others see you and thus firm up your concept of your dominant management style.

6 —

Adjusting Your Management Style

ADJUSTING a style may be more or less difficult, but in very few cases is it impossible. Modification of the stylistic approach is not in the same category as asking a leopard to change his spots.

Some managers make the mistake of thinking that a change in style can't be effected without a change in one's basic nature. This is not the case. A manager can retain his fundamental character—indeed, he cannot avoid retaining it—but, if he is conscious of the need to adopt a different style, he can alter the things he does and the way he does them to considerable advantage.

Take the example of the manager who really doesn't like people, and who has translated his dislike into a despotic style. That style has not been overly harmful during the early stages of his career, but now the executive moves into a role in which the despotic style simply won't work.

Can he learn to like people? Probably not, but that isn't even necessary. The writer and consultant Peter Drucker says of such a manager, "He will never change his fundamental nature—he is still a son of a bitch—but at least he can learn to say 'Good Morning.' "

Learning to say "good morning" is not a change in nature; it is a modification of behavior. Psychologists recognize that people who deliberately change their behavior over a sufficient period of time often wind up with fundamentally changed attitudes. This phenomenon showed up during the time when companies were hiring large numbers of minority group workers.

It became apparent that the foremen and supervisors—the key people in the process—were, on the whole, heavily biased. The companies made it clear to the foremen that it was a job requirement for them to treat the minority workers fairly. On the whole, the foremen did so, although they may not have liked it. Follow-up studies have shown that a lot of supervisors who first merely "role-played" an attitude of fairness toward minority workers ended up actually espousing such attitudes. Altered behavior can have a feedback effect.

But this does not have to happen. The manager who changes his style to adapt to a changed job situation does not have to overhaul all his opinions. Nor is this any more hypocritical than motivating an insecure subordinate by praising a certain accomplishment a little more than the objective facts would warrant.

Of course some people never change. A few managers are so confirmed in a certain kind of style that they simply cannot make any alteration. There are people in executive positions who start out as bastards and who remain bastards throughout their careers. I have known some who have driven colleagues to the point of suicide. Such people, when they possess collateral gusts of energy and decisiveness (and a little bit of luck), can go a long way. But they are hated and feared, and there is some question as to how much satisfaction they derive from their own success.

Most managers who have the objectivity to step back and evaluate their own styles have the capacity to modify those styles for the better. The key is self-interest. The manager who confronts the fact that his consensus style is not working will have to move in the direction of a better leadership style or he is through.

It is not enough to give mere lip service to a stylistic change. It must penetrate below the skin. A superficial modification that does not result in a different and better way of providing leadership is not meaningful. I have seen many examples of the unsuccessful "cosmetic" style change. Typically, a despotic manager realizes that his tendency to crack the whip over people is driving them away and robbing the enterprise of independent thought and initiative. So he forces himself to smile; he strives to keep his cool instead of blowing up; but he still pushes people around ruthlessly. This is not a real change in style.

The executive who wants to adopt a leadership style must display integrity. A surface pretense of sincerity won't work, because integrity is something you either have or don't have. It is not enough to pretend to listen to the suggestions of subordinates and vaguely promise to act on them. To become a true leader may require considerable study and research of the economics of the business, operating performance, and competitive condition.

Modification of style is a matter of self-management. The executive first understands that style is an important element in his job performance. He researches. He examines his own style so that he understands it, and he observes the styles of others. He sizes up his present style against the realities of the current situation, and faces up to the sometimes difficult task of self-criticism.

Once the manager has spotted the deficiencies in his style, he works to change it. The ideal toward which he will want to move is a pure leadership style; but, since style must match up with individual qualities, the manager should be practical rather than visionary in choosing the style that is right for him.

Some managers
can change their style.

Modifying one's style requires intelligent effort. It may be one of the most useful projects that a manager undertakes, because it can be the single most important factor in making him a more effective executive.

How does the executive detect the need for a modification in his style? How does he become aware that his style may be detrimental to the company and to himself?

Stylistic deficiencies are often difficult for the manager to understand and accept. We frequently take our styles for granted, as being an integral and unchangeable part of our makeup. The executive who takes this view would no more think of changing his style than he would think of changing his legs.

There is another factor. The manager who has achieved a measure of success has gained self-confidence and is apt to attribute problems and setbacks to outside forces rather than to deficiencies within himself. So, even though things may not be going well, he concludes that his management style is fine, and that there is no reason to change.

And then there are the managers (a distinct minority) who are very unsure of themselves. These people are only too conscious of their shortcomings. In fact, they tend to magnify them. Often they are fearful about even considering a change in style because they assume it to be a vast undertaking involving a total psychic overhaul.

Not so. Modification of management style is not all that difficult, but it can't be accomplished until the executive is able to see the signs that his present style does not fit the requirements of his job. If he keeps his eyes and ears open, there are a number of ways by which he can spot these indications.

Attitudes of Subordinates

Harry Marvin had always been a manipulator. One of the things that had made him successful was his easy-going personality. Marvin was friendly. He seemed to be approachable. He appeared to listen to subordinates when they came to him with problems or suggestions.

In truth, Marvin was not really approachable. His tendency was to make up his mind beforehand and then manipulate subordinates into believing that they were participating in decisions. Marvin had surrounded himself with people who were either easy to fool or who didn't care very much about independence as long as the paycheck arrived regularly. Marvin held lots of meetings at which his people were encouraged to "speak up." He was a facile and friendly conversationalist, and so he got along well with his team even though he was pulling the strings to make them operate as marionettes.

This approach worked all right for a while. It worked until Marvin was promoted to a level of serious responsibility. Now he had more subordinates reporting to him. Many of them had already established track records attesting to high levels of capability.

Harry Marvin set out to manipulate these people in the same fashion that he had always used. He held meetings; he encouraged expression of opinion; he engaged in friendly talk. But results were disappointing. The approach that had worked in a limited sphere was not panning out when it was used in a position of greater scope.

Marvin, an intelligent manager, wondered if it was his style that might be at fault. In thinking about the way he worked with people he did not use the term "manipulative"—but he was perceptive enough to realize that he did like to make up his mind in advance and then persuade others that they had been involved in the setting of policy.

In a review of his relationships with his key employees, particularly those who had recently come under his aegis, Marvin could not detect any serious indications of unfriendliness or resentment. People still talked with him in a friendly way. He was always able to exchange a few cordial words with everyone on his staff without feeling any strain.

Marvin might have stopped there, concluding that there was nothing wrong with his style. Wisely, he did not stop there. He thought more about his relationships with subordinates, and an interesting point occurred to him. In his dealings with people, especially those who were not handpicked members of his original team, most of the conversation was on a friendly but superficial level. He was getting along well with subordinates—but they were not talking with him about serious problems or coming to him with important suggestions. The atmosphere was always cordial, but this wasn't enough.

Reflecting on the evidence, Marvin decided that his subordinates were not talking with him about important matters because they saw no point in it. They figured that he would do as he wished anyway.

So Marvin concluded that he would have to modify his style away from manipulation and toward a genuine leadership approach. This would not be easy, but he had accomplished the first important step in that direction.

The attitude of subordinates toward a manager can tell him some interesting and useful things about his style. But it isn't enough just to analyze their behavior. He has to notice what they *don't* say as well as what they do say. If his people seem hesitant and uneasy around him, his style may be overly despotic. If subordinates tend to make too many decisions on their own without talking it over with him, he may be trying to manage by indecision.

In the words and attitudes of subordinates, a manager can often see a reflection of the appropriateness of his style.

Turnover

When an executive loses a valuable subordinate through resignation, his first impulse may be to blame the individual and/or the headhunters. He may also rationalize the episode by adopting a sour grapes attitude, which causes him to say (and sometimes really believe) that "Joe wasn't very good anyhow." Or he may explain the subordinate's departure to himself on economic grounds, reasoning that the other company made the man an offer he could not refuse.

When such losses are rare, there may be no great harm in self-delusion. But when a manager is faced with significant turnover, he may be kidding himself if he attributes the situation to factors outside the control he exercises as a manager. Purely economic factors and the persuasive powers of headhunters may be the principal agents, but this is not very likely. The consideration that makes good men change companies is job environment, and one of the most important components of job environment is the management style used by the boss.

The mere fact of increased turnover may be a clue to faulty management style. What can the manager do to explore the situation further?

Executives and industrial psychologists are skeptical of the value of most exit interviews, and rightly so. When an employee who has just quit sits down to talk it over with the boss, there are many things about the situation which militate against candor. The man who has quit may feel a little sheepish. He will certainly not want to further exacerbate the situation, if only because he wants to get out with the least possible boat rocking. Another factor that may cause the departing subordinate to pull his punches is the desire for good will which he may need to tap for a future recommendation. The boss may be angry; and even though he keeps a tight grip on his temper, he is not in a frame of mind that lends itself to objectivity.

However, in spite of all these difficulties, the subordinate who quits may be able to give his former chief some useful hints about management style.

If the manager conveys real empathy and does everything possible to keep the conversation calm and unpressured, the subordinate may open up to at least some degree. The fellow is unlikely to respond directly if he is asked "What was wrong here?" or "What were your problems with me?" However, if the interview is kept on a positive plane, and if it is focused on his expectations of what the new job offers, what he says (and what he does not say) may be enlightening. For example:

Executive Vice President Dan Hill is talking with one of his most promising department heads, Phil Jameson. Jameson has surprised and dismayed Hill by announcing that he is quitting to take a job with another firm. From all that Hill has learned, the new job doesn't seem to provide a fabulous increase in compensation or a marked career advance.

So Hill says, "I wish you all the luck in the world, Phil. I know that you'll be as valuable for them as you have been for us. I'm sure there are a number of attractive features about the new spot. What is it that particularly excites you?"

Jameson answers, "I've liked working here, and I've been treated very well. It just seemed like time to make a change. Over in my new job I can see a clearly laid out analysis of problems and plan of action. Their organization is very clean and flexible. I will know exactly what I'm supposed to do, and I think I can do it."

If Hill is astute enough, he can read between the lines to see an indictment of his own approach, which is management by confusion. For too long Hill has permitted overlapping responsibilities and vague allocations of authority. If he does not change this defective style, he will lose more good men, and those who remain will not function effectively.

The Board of Directors

It may be tough for the president or chief executive officer of an organization to be objective about his management style. The status and power inherent in his job tend to isolate him. He deals with the big picture. He makes long-range plans and broad-gauge decisions. Although he comes in contact with people in the lower echelons, they are naturally guarded with him. It is a fact of business life that subordinates tend to tell the boss what they think he wants to hear.

Often the president must depend on the board of directors—or, more likely, the board's executive committee—for indications that his style may not be all it should be. There was a time when directors were apt to be indifferent or less than candid about criticizing a chief executive, but today, partly as a result of the increased scrutiny by the government of the board's role and responsibilities, this tendency is diminishing.

The executive committee can be a valuable resource for the chief executive who wants to analyze the appropriateness of his own style. But the CEO must use his board this way. If he is touchy about criticism, if he responds to negative comments about himself as if the critic were breaking the rules of the club, then the president may not find out about a faulty style in time to correct it.

The alert CEO actively seeks out comment from the board. He knows that it may not be worded strongly. But if a number of board members seem to be talking about the same thing, however mildly, the CEO is well advised to listen. For example, some directors may say things like this: "Well, George, you are certainly running a tight ship. But don't you think you might be riding the production boys kind of hard?" The president who has been manifesting a despotic style should do some careful thinking if he hears such remarks from the board.

Criticism from a Superior Officer

The executive below the presidential level always has a boss with whom he interacts. The boss's style may not lead to frank, blunt criticism; but when the boss sees something wrong, or senses that something may be about to go wrong, he will usually make his feelings known.

Chester Burke is an exponent of the survival style. He is a master of office politics, adept in the use of the stiletto. Burke's jungle-fighting proclivities, combined with other qualities of drive and decisiveness, have enabled him to fight his way up the corporate ladder.

Burke's boss, President Len Miles, manages by consensus. He works by indirection to foster agreement among his subordinates. Until he has agreement, he does not say bold things or make bold moves.

Burke is deeply involved in political infighting, but Miles is not the kind of person who will come right out and say something about it. He will not say, "Chester, you've got to stop trying to stab people in the back. It's demoralizing, and it sours the atmosphere. Times are tough and you had better begin cooperating to achieve corporate objectives rather than your own." Miles won't even go so far as to say something like, "Chester, you have a lot of drive and ambition, and these are valuable qualities; but don't you feel that it might be wise to work a little more cooperatively with the other guys?"

No. What Len Miles does say is, "You handled yourself impressively at our last meeting, Chester. When Pete started to explain his idea for a new promotion campaign you did a hell of a job of demolishing him. Pete is not nearly as articulate or as fast on his feet as you are. Actually, though, I had a feeling that there might be something in what Pete says, as full of holes as it might be. Do you think there might be some point in our trying to draw such ideas out, instead of squelching them by throwing a lot of criticism right off the bat?"

What the president is saying, in his indirect way, is this: "Your ambition and your jungle-fighting are starting to work against the good of the company and against your own good. You'd better do something about it, or you will lose out."

The boss doesn't always comment directly on inappropriate style. He may try to concentrate on saying something positive. But, even when he seems to be uttering praise, if that praise is for things that aren't directly connected to the achievement of organizational goals, then the manager on the receiving end should pay careful attention. He is receiving a message that his style is not a good one for that situation.

Studying the Styles of Other Executives

Sometimes the manager can learn some interesting and valuable facts about his own style—what it is and what it should be—by observing other managers.

I once asked Norton Simon why he chose Dave Mahoney to head up Norton Simon, Inc. Mr. Simon observed, "I liked the way he got things done at Canada Dry and how he handled himself while getting things done. He made Canada Dry profitable. In the process he cut costs and made changes. At the same time, he continued to receive a favorable press and was well liked in the company. When a manager does an unpleasant job effectively—and is still well liked—he has a good style."

Some managers are unable to study other executives objectively. They are scornful of those who don't seem to operate well, and jealous of those who do. But the observation of successful managers is an excellent means of evaluating your own style.

Look at a manager whom you consider to be really effective. Note not just what he does, but how he does it. Identify the similarities and differences between his situation and your own. After observing the successes he has achieved, describe his management *style*. Look for the ways in which his style helps him get the job done.

The point is not to imitate a successful manager, but to learn from him.

A useful reversal of this approach is to scrutinize the executive who is *not* functioning well, obtain a sense of his style, and analyze the ways in which his style is detrimental to him. To do this we must probe deeper than the level of every-day events. It isn't enough to say, "Brown blew his chance to make a significant step up in market share because he didn't decide quickly enough on a definite course of action." This may be what happened, but *why* did it happen? Upon further analysis you may see that Brown *manages by indecision.* His failure in a critical situation is not just an aberration; it grows organically out of his management style.

One of the most productive ways of observing management style is by attending management courses and seminars, particularly those in which the participants are required to work on a problem rather than just engage in discussion. Here one can see a wide variety of styles in action. If the observer is looking for the right things, he can gain some valuable insights into the styles of others and can translate the experience into sound judgments about his own style.

Talking with Friends

Sometimes an executive can form a picture of his style, and how well it's working, by talking with a friend. This, however, is by no means the best method of self-evaluation. Good friends see you in a favorable light and they make allowances for faults. And they don't like to be critical.

Nevertheless, discussion with friends can be constructive if you know how to use it. In trying to use the reactions of a friend as a yardstick to measure your style, look for small hints. Read between the lines and note the things a friend does *not* say, the topics he steers clear of. For instance, an executive asks a long-time friend what he thinks of the manager's ability to relate to people. The friend says, "Well, you're not in business to win a popularity contest; the big thing is to get the job done." This is all well and good, and may even be largely true; but if the friend is saying it to avoid making a negative comment, he may be indicating that there is a defect in style.

Friends can be helpful; but they should not be the sole or main source of insight on executive style.

Trained Counselors

Once there was a great stigma attached to talking with a psychiatrist. The manager who did so tried desperately to keep it to himself, lest friends and colleagues think that he was on the verge of a nervous breakdown.

Fortunately our attitudes have broadened, and now psychologists, psychiatrists, and other professionals are used in industry. Some companies maintain full-time staff people trained in psychiatric disciplines. Others retain them on a regular or ad hoc basis. Management benefits from the skill and training of such professionals in a variety of ways. Some companies use them primarily in the screening and evaluation process. In other companies psychologists or psychiatrists perform more extensive diagnostic and therapeutic services. A growing number of organizations offer full-scale psychiatric counseling services, and encourage their employees—particularly their management people—to make use of it.

A trained counselor may be the ideal person for a manager to talk with about his style. Because the professional is schooled to be a dispassionate observer he can often detect strong and weak points in style which escape the manager himself, his colleagues, and his subordinates.

Psychological counseling may not be for everybody. But the executive who would like to analyze and perfect his style in order to do his job more effectively may benefit greatly from professional consultation.

———————

The manager who comes to an understanding of his own style has taken a large step forward in his career. Most of us are inclined to believe what is most flattering about ourselves. Most of the people who are closest to us are apt to tell us the things we want to hear. So it's not easy to analyze one's own style, and that's why it's important to seek several objective sources for information.

The wider you cast your net in looking for insight into your style, the better your analysis will be. You can ask for advice and comment from such sources as your public accounting firm, your advertising agency, a past employee who is a friend, a psychologist, or a management consultant.

7 -

How Your Boss's Style Helps—or Hurts—You

MANY factors determine the success or failure of an executive career. One important factor, which does not always receive appropriate attention, is the interaction of styles between boss and subordinate.

"Getting along with the boss" is not just a matter of cordial relations. Some managers have achieved enormous successes because their own management styles fitted in well with those of their superiors. Other managers, equally capable, are slowed, sidetracked, or even destroyed because of a poor stylistic matchup.

This chapter, then, is addressed to the question of harmony of styles between the ambitious executive and his superior. The aspiring manager should, in considering a job, ask himself how well his style will work with that of the person to whom he will be reporting. The other side of the coin, of course, is that the boss should ask himself equivalent questions when he is considering the hiring or promotion of a subordinate.

The problem of stylistic mates and mismates doesn't arise only at the point when a man takes a new job. Styles and circumstances change. A boss-subordinate relationship that worked well three years ago may not be working so well today. A stylistic incompatibility can easily take some time to surface. This chapter can be useful in self-evaluation and review whenever difficulties arise.

Within the next few pages we will consider each of the predominant management styles and suggest the kinds of boss-subordinate matchups that are apt to work well—or poorly. The reader will get full benefit of the suggestions if he goes in with an evaluation of his own style, based on the material in previous chapters, and an idea of the predominant style represented by his present boss or the boss he is thinking of working under.

Sometimes there is not enough information on which to base a decision about whether a certain person will be a good or a bad boss for you. However, it's wise to seek as much information as possible, and at least to avoid going to work for a man whose style is absolutely wrong for you.

The judgments rendered here are designed to serve as guidelines and thought provokers. This is not a mathematically precise checklist that will enable you to add up some numbers and emerge with an objective determination of potential success or failure. As Peter Drucker remarked, if "scientific" were synonymous with "quantified," astrology would be the queen of sciences. This material is written to help the reader to think, not to serve as a substitute for thinking.

As we comment on style, it is well to keep in mind that most subordinates are lucky if they are able to work for a true leader, a boss who can evaluate and balance the contributions of his people and bring out the best in everyone. This is not, however, universally true. We will note the exceptions.

There is one other general point that should be made. Styles may be complementary, supplementary, antithetical, or identical, and there is no rule about what combinations work well. In some situations, and for some people, supplementary styles work best together. Occasionally, antithetical styles produce the best results for superior and subordinate. It is rare, however, that the best matchup involves identical styles. For example, the manager who is predominantly a methodical, by-the-numbers operator is probably not well situated when he works for a boss whose style is just about the same. They may hit it off personally—at least for

Without a variety of styles,
management would be boring.

a time—but the results in terms of performance and career advancement are apt to be less than ideal.

With these points in mind, let's examine the styles we have identified and see what kinds of bosses they go best with. In addition to the major styles listed earlier, we will comment on two sub-styles: the instinctive approach, which is an offshoot of the creative style, and intellectual arrogance, a form of despotism. In terms of boss-subordinate relationships they warrant separate treatment.

We have not included leadership style in this listing. The fact is that a true leader is practically always a good person to work for. If your shortcomings are so serious that you would *not* want to work for a leader, then perhaps you should not be in business at all.

How about the leader who is still making his way upward? A man with leadership qualities will work well with most bosses. Of course there will be problems. The detail manager will misunderstand him; the survivor will fear him—and so forth. But the leader will do all right under almost any boss.

The Inactive Style

If you are inclined to be passive, it is essential that you give careful thought to finding the right niche.

You have little or no future if your boss is creative. He wants ideas. Furthermore, being an idea man himself, he needs subordinates who will translate ideas into action.

Don't work for a manipulator. The manager who avoids action is usually an easy mark for manipulation and comes off poorly in the confrontations entailed in such a relationship.

And the invisible boss is not for you. His invisibility calls for activist subordinates.

The executive who manages by detail may offer some possibilities. His slowness to move will, for a time, fit in with your disinclination to move. But the methodical manager does finally act, and he is apt to look askance at the subordinate who proceeds even more slowly than he does.

Your chances are fair with the consensus manager, whose pace and technique you may find congenial. Curiously, you may find it best to work for a despot or a rejector. The despot wants to take all the action himself in any case, and the rejector will turn down most proposals made to him, so your proclivity for inaction will dovetail with the effect—if not the method—of his approach.

The Detail Style

If your basic approach to business problems is the painstaking and patient accumulation of data, there are certain kinds of bosses for whom you should not work. In general, they can be classed as activists. A superior who espouses the creative style may occasionally make use of your results, but he is not likely to hold them in high regard. The despot will find you an easy target.

Don't go to the other end of the spectrum and

work for an inactive executive. His lack of energy and your inevitable slowness will result in failures of implementation that will harm both of you.

However, the invisible manager may be a good choice. Howard Hughes, the archetype of the style of invisibility, was an assiduous absorber of information collected by methodical subordinates. You can also fit in well with the consensus manager; your contributions will be of great assistance to him in his search for consensus.

You may fit well into the manipulator's pattern of playing one executive off against another.

The Invisible Style

Some kinds of bosses will permit you to follow through on your tendency to fade into the background. For example, an executive whose style is one of inactivity will find your unobtrusiveness harmonious with his method. If you work for a rejector, you will not be particularly bothered by his predilection for nay-saying. Perhaps the best choice for you would be a survivor, because you offer no threat to him. You can do all right with the methodical manager. As long as you feed him information, he will not require you to be prominently out in front.

It is not a particularly good idea to work for the creative manager. You will not feel comfortable with the idea-oriented give and take that is part of his intellectual and emotional makeup.

The consensus manager and the manipulator

are unlikely to be the kinds of bosses under whom you can flourish. The seeking of consensus and the confrontational aspects of the manipulative method both involve a considerable amount of visibility.

The despot is worst of all for you. He wants and needs visible subjects; you do not fill the bill.

Look first for a boss who is inactive or who manages by detail. Stay away from the consensus-seeker, the manipulator, and the despot.

The Consensus Style

If this is your style, you find safety in numbers. You don't feel comfortable when you are out there alone on a limb.

You will function well with the detail manager; you will not become impatient at his painstaking collection of data. You are apt to handle yourself effectively with the boss who manages by rejection; he will be lopping off the more extreme contributions of other executives, and you will have a chance to do what you do best, work within the middle range for acceptable solutions.

You may fit easily into the plans of the manipulator, because you are not hard to manage. And you will be happier with the despot than a lot of other men would be.

The survivor can be a good boss for you, because you don't make waves. He will not see your approach as a threat.

Should you work for the intellectually arrogant

boss? Maybe so, maybe not. He will not set great store on your efforts in behalf of consensus, but he may rely on it.

As for the invisible manager, you are well advised to stay away from him. The wide-open freedom he allows is less an opportunity than a burden to you.

The instinctive or creative boss is bad news; he scorns consensus, and so your long suit will have no effect.

This category offers an example of the situation in which it is advisable to seek a boss with an identical rather than complementary style. By working for a consensus manager you will be able to feel at home and enjoy maximum opportunity to do what you do best.

The Manipulative Style

The manipulator should be particularly careful in selecting the kind of boss for whom he works.

The consensus manager is a good choice. The process of gaining agreement offers a wide field of maneuver. While you do not have all the strings in your hands, your skill and inclination for handling people will count heavily in a consensus atmosphere.

The creative boss often needs a manipulator to help him execute his ideas. You have a good chance to become the strong right arm of such a superior.

If the boss is inactive or invisible, you will probably have considerable scope for your operations. However, it is well to be cautious; the lack of positive direction from the top may tempt you into excesses of manipulation that can backfire when you are not in command.

A boss who manages by rejection will cut down on your scope for manipulation by negating many of the results of your efforts.

Try to avoid the boss who manages by detail. You can manipulate people but not facts. And the despot will crush you.

If you are lucky enough to find a boss who manages by survival—and you are hard-boiled enough to take advantage of the opening—you can manipulate him right out of his job.

The Rejection Style

If you are a rejector, there are some interesting factors to consider in terms of your matchup with the kind of boss who is best for you.

You are not apt to be happy if you work for a consensus manager. The essence of consensus is the seeking of agreement. Since your inclination runs counter to that, your contributions will be seen as negative.

The survivor will mistrust you. He will take your negative attitude as being dangerous. The despot will not sanction your tendency to say no. The manipulator will victimize.

You are probably well advised to avoid working for an inactive or invisible manager; your negative tendencies will combine with those of the inactive boss to produce a lamentable lack of action, and the invisible executive tends to need subordinates with a more positive approach.

You may work quite well with a boss who manages by detail. Your practice of saying no until you are satisfied complements his drive for voluminous documentation.

The best boss for you might be a creative manager. He needs a balance wheel. He may be inclined to move too quickly, and your dampening tendency can make the two of you an effective team.

The Survival Style

Survival is rarely the route to the top, although we do occasionally find exponents of this style up there. More often than not they displayed another style during the climb, switching over to the survival approach in an effort to cling to the pinnacle.

If this is your style, you are to be congratulated for having the objectivity to identify it. There is nothing intrinsically wrong with this or any other style. The important thing is to recognize reality and act on it.

The managers who are most likely to be good bosses for the survivor are those with the following styles: methodical, despotic, manipulative, and consensus. Within the realms of each of these executives, the person who is just trying to do his job and cope should find a niche.

The survivor may have trouble with the intellectually arrogant manager and the rejector, but since he is not apt to be overly sensitive, he may do well with either.

He should not work for an invisible boss. The top man's absence from the scene places too much of a premium on individual contribution. Instinctive and creative bosses have little use for the survivor. If he is unfortunate enough to work for either, he is in real trouble.

The best to look for: detail, despotic, manipulative, consensus. Avoid the invisible, creative, and instinctive.

The Despotic Style

On the way to the top, the despot has a distinct problem. He cannot give full vent to his authoritarian tendencies until he arrives. Therefore, his choice of a boss—to the degree that he has a choice—is important.

The despot is likely to fare poorly when he works for a consensus manager. The need for consensus imposes the obligation of getting along with others, not ordering them around. The despot will simply not blend into a consensus organization.

The intellectually arrogant boss will clash too strongly with the budding despot, and so will the rejector. The instinctive manager generally forms rapid opinions about people as well as about problems. He and the despot will not get along.

The creative executive may or may not be a

good superior. If the despot's contributions are worthwhile, the creative boss will overlook other things.

The rising despot should look for the boss who is inactive or invisible. His tendency to tell people what to do may complement the inertia of the inactive executive. The detail manager may not like the despot much, but he may come to depend on his qualities of forcefulness and his ability to be ruthless in executing plans. And the despot's style may be welcome to the manipulator, who likes to set up confrontations. In a confrontation the despot will often come off pretty well.

Probably the best bet for the despot is to get into his own business as quickly as possible. However, until he is able to do this, he should evaluate his bosses carefully. Stay away from the instinctive, consensus, and rejector bosses. Look for manipulative, inactive, and invisible bosses.

The Creative Style

Creativity involves risks, so you will want a boss who will permit you to take them.

The manager by detail, who relies on the amassing of information, is wrong for you. You will never be able to offer him enough documentation.

Working for the consensus boss will not be fruitful. The essence of the creative style is that you have great confidence in your ideas and want to see them inplemented. Under the consensus-maker, they will lose their individuality and be mingled into one bland porridge of agreement.

The rejector will say no too often for you to be happy or productive with him.

Be careful about the instinctive boss. If you don't have too much personal friction with him, the matchup may be an excellent one. His instincts will incline him to support your creative concoctions.

It's never altogether nice to work for someone who is intellectually arrogant. However, this kind of boss may well have considerable—if grudging and unacknowledged—respect for your creative powers, and the frictional interaction will light off new sparks.

You may do very well if you work for a despot—if only because nobody else can work for him. You have enough confidence in your own ability to stand up to him and not to be hurt by his tyranny.

Be cautious about the manipulator. He will value your creativity only insofar as it suits his scheming mind.

The survivor is not a good boss for the creative man; he will turn down ideas that are too creative. You will, however, be able to find creative freedom under the inactive or invisible executive.

So look for the despot, inactive, and invisible. Don't work for the detail, consensus, rejection, or survival manager.

The Intellectually Arrogant Style

If you are basically contemptuous of other people, you have some obvious problems of adjustment in an organization. Nevertheless, there are spots into which you may fit and prosper.

You should not work for a despot—the constant conflict will produce little that is positive. Nor will you do well with a manipulator; your unwillingness to win friends makes you too easy a setup for him.

You will be highly frustrated by the consensus manager, and even more so, if possible, by the rejector.

The inactive manager may depend on you as long as you perform brilliantly, but you won't fit well into his overall approach. The creative or instinctive manager focuses more heavily on contribution than on personality, so he may be a good bet.

The detail manager may not be bothered too much by your contempt as long as you feed him data. The survivor—if you help him cope—will put up with your evident scorn.

Perhaps the best solution for you is to have an invisible boss. He is not around, so the chances of personality conflict are minimized, and you will be judged by your performance.

The Instinctive Style

If your instincts are reasonably sound, you may work very well with a manipulator. He is absorbed in playing one person off against another, but he acknowledges that things must be done. An instinctive subordinate assures him that things will get done. Furthermore—and you must be prepared for this—the instinctive style will make you a focus for criticism and resistance from those who are more cautious. This sort of controversy is welcome to the manipulative manager.

It may surprise you to learn that you can be a good stylistic match with the man who manages by rejection. Because his inclination is to say "no," he may serve as a useful balance wheel. You can feel freer to indulge in imaginative flights if you know that the boss will throw out your wilder schemes. However, this matchup is contingent on your willingness to accept rejection or some tempering of your suggestions so that they won't seem too far out.

The instinctive executive may complement a methodical boss to a degree that produces effective results. The rub here will always be timing—you will want to act before he is ready to.

Don't work for a consensus manager. Your urge to move will be buried in the "averaging" process. You are well advised, also, to steer clear of the inactive and invisible bosses. They just won't give you the scope you need.

The creative boss may be okay for you. Certainly in many ways your styles are congenial. However, watch out for the rivalry that is apt to grow between you.

You will be given quite a free hand if you work for a survivor, but if things go wrong he will choose you as a scapegoat. Stay away from the intellectually arrogant boss. He will not only be unpleasant to work for, but he will attack you where you are weakest.

8 ~

Making Your Style Work for You

ONCE you have come to a reasonably accurate understanding of your own style, you will want to explore ways in which you can modify it to serve you better. If you're like most executives, you're apt to find that, while certain changes are possible, it is often impossible and undesirable to try to remake yourself over into a whole new style.

*A successful style
is not always obvious.*

So you do what can be done to make your style—whatever it is—work for you. Here are some suggestions about how to do that, keyed to various styles of management.

Inaction

If you are constitutionally inclined against taking action, the most important step is to accept this fact about yourself. It does not make you a bad person. Furthermore, it is perfectly possible for people who are not dynamic activists to lead happy and profitable lives.

However, it must be admitted that the non-activist finds it difficult to cope with the pace and demands of modern management. If an inactive manager finds himself in a job requiring strong and fast action, he should do everything possible to identify those decisions that *have* to be made—and force himself to make them.

Another way to assure at least a certain amount of action is to hire people who *are* willing to act, and to delegate to them enough authority to enable them to move when it is vital.

The executive who manages by inaction—and who still enjoys a certain amount of flexibility in his career—should try to get into an area where decisiveness is not important. He may possess valuable resources of experience that can be immensely useful to other managers who have the inclination to act fast but not the wisdom to act effectively. It may be that the inactive executive would be most valuable in a staff capacity where he offers counsel without carrying the burden of follow-through.

The manager by inaction should resist the fashionable temptation to "go where the action is." He is unlikely to be either happy or successful in a high-pressure, fast-moving industry. There are some slow-moving but profitable businesses where very few management decisions are required in the course of a year, and that kind of company is best for him.

Detail

The exponent of the methodical style has certain advantages. He is thorough, he does not overlook details, he covers all bases; his decisions, when he makes them, may not be bold and sweeping, but they will be buttressed by facts.

His problem is that he is apt to act too late. There are always more data that can be collected, thereby delaying the moment of truth.

The methodical manager should devote some of his painstaking carefulness to studying this tendency in himself and building safeguards against it. There are certain things he can do to make his style more effective.

For one thing, he can look for work in areas where his hunger for data and his command of detail is a genuine advantage. An industry in which everyone knows everything that's important is not for him; it minimizes his strength. He is far better off in a job where there is always a lot of complex information to be absorbed.

The methodical manager can help himself to take the broader view at times by arranging deliberate breaks in his routine. His day-in, day-out schedule involves him with minutiae. He is always prone to the temptation to get overinvolved in detail. So, every now and then, he will do well to get away from the office and all the sources of data and just think. One thing to think about is the difference between low and high priority decisions. He can try a little hunch-playing on low priority decisions. Maybe he'll like it!

When a manager whose style is methodical becomes aware that an important decision will have to be made, he should impose on himself a deadline for action and thoroughly commit himself to it. This is the cutoff point; beyond this, he will not allow himself to seek any more data, no matter how tempted he may be.

It is vital that this kind of manager involve his employees in his fact-finding procedures. If he takes key subordinates along with him on his methodical course he will reduce friction and emphasize to them the importance of getting all the necessary information.

It's important also to have at least one trusted subordinate who pushes hard for action. He will be a blessing, because his urgings toward action are a welcome contribution to the overall functioning of the team.

With the proper balances and safeguards, management by detail can be given a sufficient dimension of action.

Invisibility

The executive who makes himself invisible does so out of a deep personal need, and there is little point in his trying to force himself to be chatty and gregarious.

However, he can arrange for certain methods of operation that can minimize the penalties of invisibility and maximize his effectiveness. He can do this in two ways.

The first is to retain several key subordinates with whom he can be comfortable and whom he can trust. They should be objective and varied enough in style and function to present, in toto, a complete view of what is going on. Moreover they must be willing to speak frankly to the invisible executive and tell him what he needs to know, the bad along with the good, even at the risk of creating some hard feelings.

It goes without saying that if he is blessed with such employees, he should listen to them. There is no other way for him to keep informed.

The other thing the invisible manager needs is to develop a comprehensive and smoothly working Management Information System. Then he can combine data from the system and his subordinates to make effective decisions.

Consensus

The consensus manager must first recognize that his ability to generate consensus is a valuable skill but not a paramount skill.

When an executive finds himself holding up action while he carries on discussions with subordinates, he is well advised to ask himself *why* he is pushing so hard for consensus. Is he sure—or reasonably sure—of what should be done, but anxious that his employees agree so that they will be vigorous and effective in carrying out the policy? Or is he using consensus as a "security blanket" because he is unsure about the proper course to take?

If the executive tries for consensus because he wants to assure willing participation in the follow-through by his staff, he must then consider that not all subordinates are alike. Some need to be brought into full agreement before they will do their best. Others, however, want the boss to give them a clear direction, and will respect the manager who does so. The proper approach, then, is to work for consensus only with those subordinates who need it.

If, on the other hand, the need for consensus grows out of insecurity, then the manager must ask himself some penetrating questions about why he is afraid to make a decision. If the fear stems from some lack in his knowledge, he should go all out to fill the gap. If it results from a general distaste to take action and responsibility, then a job requiring decisiveness is wrong for him.

There are organizations where the major contribution of the manager is to foster consensus. These are usually decentralized companies in which individual division heads enjoy considerable autonomy. It is in such a firm that the consensus manager is most appreciated.

When an executive spots in himself this tendency to seek consensus, he can protect himself from overdependence on it by setting up sensible guidelines. For example, in approaching a major decision he might conclude that 100 percent agreement is unlikely—therefore he will move when he gets substantial majority agreement. Furthermore, he should distinguish those decisions that can truly benefit by the consensus approach from those only the top man can make.

Above all, the consensus manager must determine that, beyond a certain point, the search for agreement must never be allowed to hold up desired action.

Manipulation

The manipulative style can work well if the manager who uses it is aware of its limitations and of the guidelines within which it should be applied.

It is extremely important that the manipulator begin with a clear set of objectives. He should understand fully the goals of the organization and set up sub-goals for himself that conform with overall objectives. Manipulation is futile at best and destructive at worst unless it is applied toward clearly defined goals.

Manipulation does not build a strong staff. The

manager who works through this style should learn that he must not look for brilliance and ingenuity in his subordinates, because his approach will either diminish these attributes in the people who work for him or impel them to leave.

Manipulation in pursuit of positive goals is acceptable—if it works and keeps on working. The kind of manipulation that causes conflict is almost always harmful.

The manipulative manager has to face the fact that he will always have to be able to do all the important things himself; he is not building people who can gradually take over some of his responsibilities. This style is best deployed in a business requiring good results *now,* without much regard for growth. It exacts from its practitioners great resources of energy and demands that they give an enormous amount of personal attention to the business.

Rejection

There is not much good that can be said about management by rejection. The executive who detects in himself a tendency to say no to everything should seek an area of operation that does not call upon him to make and carry out large plans, nor to manage superior people.

The chronic rejector's best—and probably only—arena is a long-established enterprise in which the premium rests on maintaining the status quo and saving money. He is most valuable to an organization that is struggling to survive and must watch every penny, but since few careers can be built on such foundations, management by rejection is rarely the path to the heights.

When the executive whose basic style is rejection finds himself in a position that calls for at least occasional positive action, he should support himself with a key assistant who is his alter ego—enthusiastic, adventurous. He should bestow confidence and responsibility on this subordinate and try to manage things so that he and his associate balance each other in producing careful but positive decisions.

This manager is probably not a pure rejector. His approach contains traces of other styles. If, for example, he finds in himself a slight tendency toward inaction, the rejector should try to move in this direction by delaying proposals rather than rejecting them immediately.

Survival

When an executive makes the tough, objective self-judgment that his style is one of survival, he is to be commended for his honesty. This is a hard thing to face. Realistically, however, there are many people in high positions whose basic instinct is that of survival. Those who recognize it in themselves have done themselves a service provided they are willing to act on their insight.

The survivor is not a leader. He should therefore avoid positions that call for qualities of individual leadership. Such positions are, for him, overly exposed. He will not handle them well and his chances of survival will be reduced.

An executive whose style is that of survival should look for a subordinate job under a good leader. He should develop to the utmost his skills on the job. Furthermore, he should make himself a reservoir of advice and support for his boss. The only sure way to survive is through indispensability; and a manager becomes indispensable by developing an unmatched ability to do a certain job better than anyone else can do it. In developing such abilities, he is best situated in an organization large and stable enough to value the consistent performer who is not a "tiger" and who will never become chairman of the board.

The executive who strives for survival by attacking others is in a losing game. It is only a matter of time until he himself is cut down.

Despotism

The most important thing for the managerial despot to remember is that he must continue to be decisive and totalitarian in his actions—once he has established himself as a despot. Whether he is a benevolent despot or a destructive one, he cannot permit himself the luxury of relaxing and becoming "Mr. Nice Guy" once he has achieved a position of responsibility.

He can't change. He cannot begin to delegate

important decisions that he previously arrogated to himself. He has not built a staff of subordinates who have the personal strength and will to make decisions on their own. They are conditioned to carry out the despot's decisions—and he had better be sure they are the right ones. He has, without doubt, made enemies who will be just waiting for a sign of weakness.

So the despot must place a high premium on having the most accurate and up-to-date information that he can get—on the economy, the industry, the competition, the state of the company, and so forth.

The executive who runs things in the despotic style should be careful to pay people well and to reward them in other ways for good work in carrying out his unilateral decisions. He cannot expect to keep independent and ambitious subordinates on his payroll, but he needs effective people to implement his policies.

If possible, the despot will benefit by altering his style in the direction of consensus—or, perhaps, invisibility. A tyrant is less offensive when you don't see him so often.

The despot whose specialty is intellectual arrogance should seek a business in which human relations are not very important. Such a spot might be found in a highly technical company or a process industry. However, no matter how far the intellectually arrogant manager goes to insulate himself from people, he can never entirely do without them.

There is no business in which human relations can be avoided altogether, or in which arrogance is of great advantage. Therefore, although he may never abandon his feeling of superiority, he should at least learn to have respect for the opinions of others.

Creativity

The possessor of the creative style of management is a creature of instinct. His long suit is ideas. He may not be effective at the more methodical functions of translating ideas into action.

This manager should surround himself with capable administrators. He will not call on them for creativity equal to his own, but he will acknowledge that they possess valuable skills in getting things done. In consideration of this, the creative manager functions best when he monitors his subordinates for results rather than trying to control each action.

Highly creative people need a balance wheel. The creative manager will get best results by listening to subordinates when they produce evidence to show that too much innovation will have a bad effect on profits.

One of the principal pitfalls that the creative manager has to watch out for is his tendency to become so attached to a pet idea that he refuses to drop it in the face of staff opposition and data that cast doubt on its feasibility. It is much better to go on to another idea—and it is more fun as well.

The creative manager tends to give his instincts free rein on all decisions, including those related to personnel. Here he is well advised to be careful. An executive whose "feel" is unparalleled in discerning market trends may not be very perceptive in judging people. Furthermore, since personnel decisions rarely have to be made in a hurry, the creative manager should take all the time he needs to be sure his decisions are sound. The careful selection of subordinates is extremely important to the creative executive, because he must turn over a great deal of administration to them.

Leadership

The manager who is fortunate enough to be gifted with a leadership style can maintain his advantage by sitting back, from time to time, and remembering what made him a leader. He has the ability to listen, to respect others, to get at the root of problems. He is able to draw correct conclusions from data, make decisions, and get employees to work willingly toward company goals.

Occasional self-review is important. Leaders tend, after a time, to move toward the despotic style. They know that their opinions and decisions are usually correct but this knowledge may lead them to become overconfident. When a manager begins to lose respect for subordinates, he starts to turn into a despot.

A true leadership style is too valuable to lose. The leader need never lack self-confidence; people are anxious to follow him. Part of the essence of his

leadership lies in his sensitivity and his consideration for people as well as his grasp of trends and
events. Periodic review of the principles and qualities of leadership will serve to maintain the leadership style.

9 –

Finishing Up in Style

IN this excursion through the world of style in management we have not seen anything new in the way of executive behavior. We have, however, looked at the vital matter of management success/failure from a new perspective.

We have seen how an organization can go downhill when it is run by a man with the wrong style,

153

and how it can turn around when the right style of management comes into play.

We have seen how an executive can overcome career problems by understanding and modifying his style, or by finding the job in which his style is most effective. We have viewed the spectrum of management styles, observed them in action, considered the means by which a defective style can be spotted and perhaps remedied. And we have noted that a style is not necessarily intrinsically good or bad. It is in the matchup of style with job that success or failure is determined.

The first thing I hope the reader will take away from this book is a consciousness of the existence of style in management. Everyone has a style. The mere recognition of that fact can be of considerable value in itself.

Having seen that style is a factor in executive functioning, the reader is led to ask, "How important is it?" By means of case histories and analyses, I have tried to demonstrate the importance of the subject. But the reader may draw his own conclusions from observation.

One can best begin to see how style works— and the effects it has—by observing it in others, notably subordinates. Look at managers. Observe them in their everyday activities. Watch them perform under stress. Define the particular style, or combination of styles, that the individual brings to bear on his tasks, his problems, his relationships. When you look for it, you can begin to judge how well a management style works in getting things done.

From this observation of style in others, the

manager can work back toward a better understanding of his own stylistic approach. In thinking over the way he handled a situation he can ask himself, "What style did I use in this instance?" bearing in mind that style is not experience, or intelligence, or personality, or courage, but rather the means by which the mix of these elements is applied to the job. Keep in mind our definition of management style as "a combination of characteristics, innate and acquired, that indicates what a man is, influences the things he does, and controls the effectiveness with which he does them."

Observation of style, in oneself as in others, must always take place in the context of the conditions and responsibilities of the job that the manager is trying to do. A certain style may serve a man well in bringing him up the ladder; but that same style may be ineffectual when he attains a position of command. On the other hand, an executive may have a style that is frustrated by the conditions in which he works at a lower level, but may be able to accomplish great things with that same style when he is given freedom and authority. It's important for him—and for the organization—to maintain a balanced perspective. A style cannot be wrenched into the shape of another style to suit current circumstances. It is better to identify the surrounding situation—the boss-subordinate matchup, the nature of the job—and determine what can be modified.

A sense of style can be an invaluable tool for the manager. He can use it to analyze the performance of others. He can take stock of his own successes and failures—and opportunities for growth—by consid-

*Different management styles
can produce the same favorable results.*

ering his own style. He can make his knowledge of style work for him in hiring and promoting people to do specific jobs. He can rely on his awareness of the importance of style—and his sensitivity to clashes in style—as a diagnostic device to penetrate to the root of problems and to predict difficulties before they become acute.

And a feeling for style is essential for the manager on the way up. Success or failure may depend largely on how he works with his boss. An assessment of the boss's style—and comparison with his own style—will give the manager a better sense of where he should be and what he can expect to accomplish.

So the concept of style in management is a valuable tool. But it is something else; it is a joy. It gives spice and variety to the executive task. Without differences in style, management would be a dull occupation. When one is attuned to its existence and its importance, he is a better manager—and he will enjoy his work more.

With the reader's indulgence, I would like to single out some of the capable executives I've been privileged to know and work with. I think their outstanding successes owe a great deal to that ubiquitous quality, style:

- Michele Ferrero, who started in his father's bakery in Turin, Italy, and built the Ferrero company into one of the world's great food and confectionery businesses through his marketing and research genius;
- Joe Grazier, who started American Standard on its suc-

157

cessful growth pattern that is being carried on by his successors;

* Leon Hess, who started as a small operator in the coal business and built one of the great oil companies of the world, Amerada Hess;
* John Kluge, who founded Metromedia and developed it into one of the world's leading communications companies;
* Harding Lawrence, who converted Braniff, a sleepy Southwest airline, into a large, successful international operation;
* Ed Little, who built the International Division of Colgate that has made Colgate-Palmolive one of the world's greatest businesses of toilet articles and household products;
* Dave Mahoney, who consolidated and expanded the great Norton Simon company;
* John Mecom, whose imagination and perseverance created one of the large oil empires in the Southwest;
* Ed Ney, who rescued a faltering Young & Rubicam and restored it to its position of greatness and beyond;
* Marion Sadler and Bill Hogan, who made American Airlines into one of the most profitable and best performers in that industry;
* Bill Seawell, who has done a most creditable job in turning around Pan American Airways from its financial plight;
* Bob Six, one of the world's outstanding airline executives, who has been Chief Executive Officer of Continental Airlines since its inception forty-two years ago and who is an amazingly dynamic and able executive;
* Mary Wells, who started an advertising agency from scratch and has expanded it into one of the country's best-known agencies with a spectacular record and excellent financial performance.

Some younger executives whose style and ability are making their mark are:

Tom Barnum of Sara Lee
Reg Brack of Time
Alex Brody and Alex Kroll of Young & Rubicam
Charlie Bucks of Continental Airlines
Dan Colussy and Bill Waltrip of Pan Am
Bob Crandall of American Airlines

Style is an essential factor in management. What may be even more important is that it makes management challenging and intriguing. Each of these executives has utilized a distinctive management style, plus tremendous talents, either to create a company or to make his company grow in unique and profitable ways. Obviously there are thousands more like them.